THE
ITALIAN
TRAVELMATE

THE
ITALIAN
TRAVELMATE

Compiled by Lexus
with Annelisa Franchini

Chronicle Books · San Francisco

First published in the United States in 1991 by
Chronicle Books.

Printed in the United States of America.

Cover design: Kathy Warinner
Composition: TBH Typecast

ISBN: 0-87701-874-X

10 9 8 7 6 5 4 3 2 1

Chronicle Books
275 Fifth Street
San Francisco, California 94103

 printed on recycled paper

YOUR TRAVELMATE
gives you one single easy-to-use list of words and
phrases to help you communicate in Italian.

Built into this list are:
– Travel Tips with facts and figures which
provide valuable information
– Italian words you'll see on signs and notices
– typical replies to some of the things you might
want to say.

There is a menu reader on pages 74–75, the
Italian alphabet is given on page 126 and
numbers on page 127.

Your TRAVELMATE also tells you how to
pronounce Italian. Just read the pronunciations
as though they were English and you will
communicate – although you might not sound like
a native speaker.

If no pronunciation is given then the word itself
can be pronounced as though it were English.
And sometimes only part of a word or phrase
needs a pronunciation guide. Vowels given in
italics show which part of a word to stress.

a, an un, una [oon, *oo*-nah]

    800 lire a litre ottocento lire al litro
    [ot-toh-chen-toh *lee*-ray . . .]

abdomen l'addome [ad-d*oh*-may]

aboard a bordo

about:

    about 15 circa quindici [ch*ee*r-kah
    kw*ee*n-dee-chee]

    about 2 o'clock verso le due [. . . d*oo*-ay]

above sopra

abroad all'estero [al-l*e*s-tay-roh]

absolutely! certo! [ch*ay*r-toh]

accelerator l'acceleratore [la-chay-lay-ra-t*oh*-ray]

accendere i fari switch on headlights

accept accettare [a-chet-t*ah*-ray]

accident un incidente [een-chee-d*e*n-tay]

    there's been an accident è successo un
    incidente [eh soo-ch*e*s-soh . . .]

accommodation un posto da dormire
    [. . . dor-m*ee*-ray]

    we need accommodation for three c'è [cheh]
    posto da dormire per tre?

» *TRAVEL TIP: information can be obtained from
the local tourist office, called "Pro Loco"*

accountant un ragioniere [ra-jon-y*eh*-ray]

accurate accurato

ache un dolore [doh-l*oh*-ray]

    my back aches mi fa mal la schiena [mee fah
    mal lah skee-*ay*-nah]

ACI = Automobile Club d'Italia: like our AAA

acqua potabile drinking water

across attraverso
   how do we get across? come attraversiamo?
   [koh-may . . .]
adapter una spina intermedia [spee-nah
   een-ter-may-dee-ah]
address l'indirizzo [een-dee-reet-tzoh]
   will you give me your address? mi dai il
   tuo indirizzo? [mee dah-ee . . .]
adhesive bandage il cerotto [chay-rot-toh]
adjust aggiustare [ah-joos-tah-ray]
admission l'entrata
advance: can we reserve in advance?
   possiamo prenotare? [. . . –tah-ray]
advertisement un annuncio [an-noon-choh]
afraid: I'm afraid I don't know purtroppo non
   so
   I'm afraid so purtroppo sì [. . . see]
   I'm afraid not no, mi spiace [no mee
   spee-ah-chay]
after: after you dopo di lei [. . . de lay]
   after 3 o'clock dopo le tre [. . . lay tray]
afternoon il pomeriggio [po-may-ree-joh]
   this afternoon questo pomeriggio
   in the afternoon nel pomeriggio
   good afternoon *(from morning till mid-*
   afternoon) buon giorno [bwon jor-noh] *(after*
   that) buona sera [bwo-nah say-rah]
aftershave il dopobarba
again ancora
against contro
age l'età [ay-tah]
   under age minorenne [mee-no-ren-nay]
   it takes ages ci vogliono anni [chee
   vol-yoh-noh an-nee]
ago: a week ago una settimana fa
   it wasn't long ago non tanto tempo fa
   how long ago was that? quanto tempo fa?
agree: I agree sono d'accordo
   it doesn't agree with me non mi fa bene [non
   mee fah bay-nay]
air l'aria (ah-ree-ah)

by air in aereo [een ah-*eh*-ray-oh]
by airmail per posta aerea [. . . ah-*eh*-ray-ah]
with air-conditioning con l'aria condizionata
[. . . kon-dee-tzee-o-n*ah*-tah]
airport l'aeroporto [ah-ay-ro-p*o*r-toh]
alarm l'allarme [–may]
   alarm clock le sveglia [sv*ay*l-yah]
alcohol l'alcole [*a*l-koh-lay]
   is it alcoholic? è alcolico? [eh al-k*o*-lee-koh]
alive vivo [v*ee*-voh]
   is he still alive? è ancora vivo? [eh . . .]
all tutto [t*oo*t-toh]
   all night tutta la notte [–tay]
   that's all wrong è tutto sbagliato
   [eh . . . sbal-y*ah*-toh]
   all right va bene [. . . b*ay*-nay]
   I'm all right sto bene
   that's all è tutto
   thank you – not at all grazie – prego
   [gr*ah*-tzee ay pr*ay*-goh]
allergic allergico [al-l*e*r-jee-koh]
   I'm allergic to sono allergico a
allowed permesso
   is it allowed? è permesso?
   it's not allowed è vietato [eh vee-ay-t*ah*-toh]
   allow me mi permetta [mee . . .]
almost quasi [k*wah*-see]
alone solo
   did you come here alone? è venuto solo?
   [eh . . .]
   leave me alone mi lasci stare [mee l*ah*-shee
   st*ah*-ray]
Alps: the Alps le Alpi [lay-*a*l-pee]
already già [djah]
also anche [*a*n-kay]
alt halt
alternator l'alternatore [–t*oh*-ray]
although sebbene [seb-b*eh*-nay]
altogether in tutto [een t*oo*t-toh]
   what does that make altogether? quant'è in
   tutto? [kwan-t*eh* . . .]

always sempre [sem-pray]
a.m. di mattina [dee mat-tee-nah]
ambassador l'ambasciatore [am-ba-sha-toh-ray]
ambulance un'ambulanza [am-boo-lan-tzah]
   get an ambulance! chiamate un'ambulanza!
   [kee-a-mah-tay . . .]
» *TRAVEL TIP: phone 113 anywhere in Italy*
America l'America [a-may-ree-kah]
American americano
among fra
anchor l'ancora [an-ko-rah]
ancient Rome Roma Antica [. . . an-tee-kah]
and e [ay]
angry seccato
   I'm very angry about it sono molto seccato
   al riguardo [. . . ree-gwar-doh]
   please don't get angry non si arrabbi [non
   see ar-rab-bee]
animal un animale [a-nee-mah-lay]
ankle la caviglia [ka-veel-yah]
anniversary: it's our anniversary è il nostro
   anniversario [eh . . .]
annoy: he's annoying me mi sta seccando
   [mee . . .]
   it's very annoying è molto seccante
   [eh mol-toh sayk-kan-tay]
another: can we have another room?
   potremmo avere un'altra camera?
   [. . . a-vay-ray . . .]
   another beer, please un'altra birra, per
   favore [. . . fa-voh-ray]
answer *(noun)* una risposta
   what was his answer? qual'è stata la sua
   risposta?
   there was no answer nessuno ha risposto
   [. . . ah . . .]
antifreeze l'antigelo [an-tee-jay-loh]
any: have you any bananas/butter? avete
   delle banane/del burro? [a-vay-tay dayl-lay
   ba-nah-nay . . .]
   I haven't got any non ne ho [non nay o]

anybody qualcuno [kwal-k*oo*-noh]
  I can't see anybody non vedo nessuno
  [. . . v*ay*-doh . . .]
anything qualcosa
  anything will do va bene tutto [vah b*ay*-nay
  t*oo*t-toh]
  I don't want anything non voglio niente [non
  vol-yoh nee-*e*n-tay]
apartment un appartamento
aperitif un aperitivo [−*tee*-voh]
aperto open
apology una scusa [sk*oo*-sah]
  please accept my apologies mi scusi
  [mee . . .]
  I want an apology desidero le sue scuse
  [day-*see*-day-roh lay s*oo*-ay . . .]
appendicitis l'appendicite [ap-pen-dee-ch*ee*-tay]
appetite l'appetito [ap-pay-*tee*-toh]
  I've lost my appetite non ho più appetito
  [. . . o pew . . .]
apple una mela
application form il modulo [m*o*-doo-loh]
**appointment: can I make an
  appointment?** posso avere un appuntamento?
  [. . . a-v*ay*-ray . . .]
apricot un'albicocca
April aprile [a-pr*ee*-lay]
archaeology l'archeologia [−j*ee*-ah]
area area [*ah*-ray-ah]
arm il braccio [br*ah*-choh]
around: is the manager around? c'è il
  direttore? [cheh eel dee-rayt-t*oh*-ray]
arrange: will you arrange it? ci pensa lei?
  [chee-pen-sah lay]
  it's all arranged è tutto a posto [eh . . .]
arrest: he's been arrested è stato arrestato [eh
  st*ah*-toh . . .]
arrival l'arrivo [ar-r*ee*-voh]
arrive arrivare [ar-ree-v*ah*-ray]
  we only arrived yesterday siamo arrivati
  solo ieri [. . . *yeh*-ree]

arrivi *arrivals*
art l'arte [ar-tay]
   art gallery una galleria d'arte
   [gal-lay-ree-ah . . .]
arthritis l'artrite [ar-tree-tay]
artificial artificiale [ar-tee-fee-chah-lay]
artist l'artista
as: as quickly as you can il più in fretta
   possibile [eel pew een frayt-tah pos-see-
   bee-lay]
   as much as you can il più che può [. . . kay
   pwoh]
   do as I do faccia come me [fah-chah koh-may
   may]
   as you like come le pare [koh-may lay
   pah-ray]
ascensore *elevator*
ashore a terra
   to go ashore sbarcare [sbar-kah-ray]
   we've run ashore siamo incagliati
   [. . . een-kal-yah-tee]
ashtray un portacenere [por-ta-chay-nay-ray]
ask chiedere [kee-ay-day-ray]
   could you ask him to do it for me? può
   chiedergli di farlo per me? [pwoh kee-ay-der-lee
   dee . . . may]
   that's not what I asked for non è quello che
   ho chiesto [. . . kay o kee-es-toh]
asleep: he's still asleep è ancora addormentato
   [eh . . .]
asparagus gli asparagi [lee as-pah-ra-jee]
aspirin un'aspirina
assistant l'assistente [–tay]
asthma l'asma
at: at the café al caffè [kaf-feh]
   at my hotel al mio albergo
atmosphere l'atmosfera
attenti al cane *beware of the dog*
attenzione *caution*
attitude l'atteggiamento [at-tay-ja-men-toh]

attractive attraente [at-tra-*e*n-tay]
  I think you're very attractive ti [tee] trovo molto attraente
August agosto
aunt la zia [tz*ee*-ah]
Australia l'Australia [ows-tr*a*l-yah]
Australian australiano [ows-tr*a*l-y*a*h-noh]
Austria l'Austria [*ow*s-tree-ah]
Austrian austriaco [ows-tr*ee*-a-koh]
authorities le autorità [ow-toh-ree-t*ah*]
automatic *(car)* un'automatica
  [ow-toh-m*ah*-tee-kah]
autostrada *freeway*
autumn l'autunno [ow-t*oo*n-noh]
  in the autumn in autunno
avanti *cross now*
away: is it far away from here? è molto
  lontano da qua? [eh . . .]
  go away! va' via! [. . . v*ee*-ah]
awful terribile [ter-*ree*-bee-lay]
axle l'asse [*a*s-say]
baby il bam*b*ino
  we'd like a baby-sitter vorremmo una baby-sitter
back: I've got a bad back ho il mal di schiena
  [o eel mal dee skee-*ay*-nah]
  I'll be back soon torno subito
  [. . . s*oo*-bee-toh]
  is he back? è tornato? [eh . . .]
  can I have my money back? posso avere
  indietro il denaro? [. . . a-v*ay*-ray
  een-dee-*eh*-troh . . .]
  come back torni indietro
  I go back tomorrow ritorno domani
  at the back dietro [dee-*eh*-troh]
backpack lo zaino [tza-*ee*-noh]
bacon la pancetta affumicata [pan-ch*ay*t-tah . . .]
  bacon and eggs pancetta e uova [. . . ay
  w*o*-vah]
bad cattivo [kat-t*ee*-voh]

it's not bad non c'è male [non cheh m*ah*-lay]
the milk/meat is bad il latte è andato/
la carne è andata a male [eel l*a*t-tay eh
an-d*ah*-toh/la k*a*r-nay eh an-d*ah*-tah ah
m*ah*-lay]
too bad! paziena! [pa-tzee-*en*-tzah]
bag una borsa; *(handbag)* una borsetta
baggage i bagagli [ee ba-gal-yee]
bagno bathroom
baker il panettiere [pa-nayt-y*eh*-ray]
balcony il balcone [bal-k*oh*-nay]
  a room with a balcony una c*a*mera con
  balcone
ball una palla
ballpoint pen una biro [*bee*-roh]
banana una banana
band *(music)* l'orchestra
bandage una benda
  could you change the bandage? può
  combiare la benda? [pwoh kam-bee-*ah*-ray . . .]
bank la banca *(river)* la sponda
» *TRAVEL TIP: banks in Italy are open from 8:30 to
1:30; "bank holidays" see* **'public holidays'**
bar il bar
  when does the bar open? quando apre il
  bar? [. . . *ah*-pray . . .]
» *TRAVEL TIP: in most bars you must pay at the
cash register before ordering and show your
ticket (scontrino) at the bar*
  YOU MAY THEN HEAR . . .
  ritiri lo scontrino alla cassa *get your ticket at
the cash register*
barbershop il barbiere [bar-bee-*ay*-ray]
bargain: it's a real bargain è proprio un affare
  [. . . af-f*ah*-ray]
bartender il barista (ba-r*ee*s-tah)
basket il cestino [ches-t*ee*-noh]
bassinet la culla portatile [k*oo*l-lah
  por-ta-t*ee*-lay]
bath il bagno [b*a*n-yoh]

can I have a bath? posso fare [fah-ray] il
bagno?

could you give me a bath towel? può darmi
un asciugamano da bagno? [pwoh dar-mee oon
a-shoo-ga-mah-noh dah . . .]

bathing suit un costume da bagno
[kos-too-may . . .]

bathrobe una vestaglia [ves-tal-yah]

bathroom il bagno [ban-yoh]

**we want a room with a private
bathroom** vorremmo una camera con bagno

can I use your bathroom? posso usare
[oo-zah-ray] il bagno?

» *TRAVEL TIP: see* **toilet**

battery una pila [pee-lah] *(car)* la batteria
[bat-tay-ree-ah]

be essere [es-say-ray]

be . . . sia . . .

don't be . . . non sia . . .

beach la spiaggia [spee-ah-jah]

see you on the beach ci [chee] vediamo in
spiaggia

let's go to the beach andiamo al mare
[. . . mah-ray]

beans i fagioli [ee fa-joh-lee]

beautiful bello

a beautiful woman una bella donna

that was a beautiful meal il pranzo era
molto buono [eel pran-tzoh eh-rah mol-toh
bwo-noh]

because perché [per-kay]

because of the weather a causa del tempo
[ah kow-zah . . .]

bed il letto

single bed/double bed letto singolo/letto
matrimoniale [. . . –ah-lay]

I want to go to bed voglio andare a dormire
[vol-yoh an-dah-ray ah dor-mee-ray]

bed and breakfast una pensione
[payn-see-oh-nay]

....

bee un'ape [*ah*-pay]

beef il manzo [m*a*n-tzoh]

beer la birra [b*ee*r-rah]

    two beers, please due birre, per favore
[d*oo*-ay b*ee*r-ray payr fa-v*oh*-ray]

before: before breakfast prima di colazione
[pr*ee*-mah dee ko-la-tzee-*oh*-nay]

    before we leave prima di partire [. . . –ray]

    I haven't been here before non c'ero mai
stato [non ch*eh*-roh m*ah*-ee . . .]

begin: when does it begin? quando inizia?
[kwan-doh ee-n*ee*-tzee-ah]

    I'm a beginner sono un principiante
[. . . preen-chee-pee-*a*n-tay]

beginner's slope *(skiing)* la pista per
principianti [p*ee*s-tah payr preen-cheep-y*a*n-tee]

behind dietro [dee-*eh*-troh]

    the car behind me l'auto dietro [ow-toh . . .]

believe: I don't believe you non la credo
[. . . kr*a*y-doh]

    I believe you la credo

bell *(in hotel, etc.)* il campanello

belong: that belongs to me mi appartiene [mee
ap-par-tee-*a*y-nay]

    who does this belong to? a chi appartiene?
[ah kee . . .]

below sotto

belt la cintura [cheen-*too*-rah]

bend *(in road)* una curva [k*oo*r-vah]

berries le bacche [b*a*k-kay]

berth *(on ship)* una cuccetta [koo-ch*a*yt-tah]

beside accanto a

best migliore [meel-y*oh*-ray]

    it's the best vacation I've ever had è la
migliore vacanza che abbia fatto
[. . . va-k*a*n-tzah kay . . .]

better meglio [m*e*l-yoh]

    haven't you got anything better? non ha
niente de meglio? [non ha nee-*e*n-tay dee . . .]

    are you feeling better? si sente meglio? [see
s*e*n-tay . . .]

I'm feeling a lot better mi [mee] sento molto meglio

between tra

beyond oltre [ol-tray]

bicycle la bicicletta [bee-chee-klayt-tah]

big grande [−day]

    a big one uno grande

    that's too big è troppo grande [eh . . .]

    it's not big enough non è grande abbastanza [. . . ab-bas-tan-tzah]

    have you got a bigger one? ne avete uno più grande? [nay a-vay-tay oo-noh pew . . .]

biglietti tickets

bikini il bikini

bill il conto

    could I have the bill, please? potrei avere il conto? [po-tray a-vay-ray . . .]

» *TRAVEL TIP: service−see* **tipping**

binario platform

binding *(skiing)* l'attacco

bird un uccello [oo-chel-loh]

birthday il compleanno [kom-play-an-noh]

    it's my birthday è il mio compleanno [eh eel mee-oh . . .]

    happy birthday buon compleanno [bwon . . .]

bit: just a bit solo un po'

    that's a bit too expensive è un po' troppo caro

    a big bit un bel pezzo

bite *(noun)* un morso

    I've been bitten sono stato punto [. . . stah-toh poon-toh] *(by dog)* sono stato morso

bitter *(taste)* amaro

black nero [nay-roh]

    he's had a blackout è svenuto

bland blando

blanket una coperta

    I'd like another blanket vorrei un'altra coperta [vor-ray . . .]

bleach la candeggina [kan-day-*jee*-nah]
bleed sanguinare [san-gwee-*nah*-ray]
   he's bleeding sanguina
bless you *(after sneeze)* salute! [-tay]
blind cieco [*cheh*-koh]
   blind spot *(driving)* zona cieca [tzo-nah . . .]
   blind: his lights were blinding me i suoi
   fari mi abbagliavano [ee swoy-ee *fah*-ree mee
   ab-bal-*yah*-va-noh]
blister una vescica [vay-*shee*-kah]
blocked bloccato
blonde una bionda [bee-*on*-dah]
blood il sangue [*san*-gway]
   his blood type is . . . il suo gruppo sanguigno
   è . . . [. . . groop-poh san-*gween*-yoh . . .]
   I've got high blood pressure ho la pressione
   alta [o lah prays-*yoh*-nay . . .]
   he needs a blood transfusion ha bisogno di
   una trasfusione [ah bee-*s*onn-yoh dee . . . -nay]
Bloody Mary un bloody mary
blouse una camicetta [ka-mee-*chayt*-tah]
blue blu
board: full board la pensione completa
   [pen-see-*oh*-nay . . .]
   half board la mezza pensione [m*et*-tzah . . .]
   boarding pass la carta d'imbarco
boat una barca
   boat train treno di coincidenza con la nave
   [. . . dee ko-een-chee-*d*en-tzah kon lah n*ah*-vay]
body il corpo *(dead body)* un morto
boil *(verb)* bollire [-ray]
   (noun) una pustola [p*oo*s-toh-lah]
   do we have to boil the water? dobbiamo
   bollire l'acqua?
   boiled egg un uovo alla coque [wo-voh *a*l-lah
   kok]
bone un osso
book un libro [l*ee*-broh]
bookstore una libreria [-*ee*-ah]
boot *(shoe)* uno stivale [stee-v*ah*-lay]
border il confine [kon-*fee*-nay]

bored: I'm bored sono annoiato [ann-no-yah-toh]

boring noioso [no-yoh-soh]

born: I was born in 1956 sono nato nel millenovecentocinquantasei
[... meel-lay-no-vay-chen-toh-cheen-kwan-ta-say]

borrow: can I borrow ...? posso avere in prestito ...? [... a-vay-ray een pres-tee-toh]

boss il capo

both entrambi [en-tram-bee]
   I'll take both of them li prendo entrambi [lee ...]

bottle una bottiglia [bot-teel-yah]

bottle opener un apribottiglia

bottom: at the bottom of the hill in fondo alla collina

bouncer il buttafuori [boot-tah-fwo-ree]

bowels l'intestino [een-tes-tee-noh]

bowl una scodella

box una scatola [skah-toh-lah]

boy il ragazzo [ra-gat-tzoh]

boyfriend: my boyfriend il mio ragazzo [mee-oh ra-gat-tzoh]; *(older)* il mio amico

bra il reggiseno [reh-jee-say-noh]

bracelet il braccialetto [bra-cha-layt-toh]

brake *(noun)* il freno [fray-noh]
   could you check the brakes? può controllare i freni? [pwoh kon-trol-lah-ray ee ...]
   I had to brake suddenly ho dovuto frenare all'improvviso [o do-voo-toh fray-nah-ray ... −vee-soh]
   he didn't brake non ha [ah] frenato

brandy un brandy

bread il pane [pah-nay]
   could we have some bread and butter? potremmo avere del pane e burro? [... a-vay-ray ...]
   some more bread, please ancora del pane, per favore [... fa-voh-ray]

break *(verb)* rompere [rom-pay-ray]

I think I've broken my arm penso d'aver rotto il braccio [. . . br*ah*-choh]

breakable fragile [fr*ah*-jee-lay]

breakdown un guasto [gw*as*-toh]

I've had a breakdown ho avuto un guasto [o . . .]

nervous breakdown l'esaurimento nervoso [ay-zow-ree-m*e*n-toh . . .]

» *TRAVEL TIP: breakdown services—phone 116*

breakfast la colazione [ko-la-tzee-*oh*-nay]

breast il petto

breath il fiato [fee-*ah*-toh]

breathe respirare [res-pee-r*ah*-ray]

I can't breathe non posso respirare

bridge il ponte [p*on*-tay]

briefcase la valigetta [va-lee-j*ay*t-tah]

brilliant *(very good)* brillante [−tay]

bring portare [por-t*ah*-ray]

could you bring it to my hotel? può [pwoh] portarlo al mio albergo?

Britain la Gran Bretagna [. . . bray-t*an*-yah]

British inglese [een-gl*ay*-say]

brochure un opuscolo [o-p*oos*-ko-loh]

have you got any brochures about . . . ? ha un opuscolo su . . . ? [ah . . .]

broken rotto

you've broken it l'ha rotto [lah . . .]

it's broken è rotto [eh . . .]

my room/car has been broken into mi hanno svaligiato la camera/l'auto [mee *an*-noh sva-lee-j*ah*-toh la k*ah*-may-rah/l*ow*-toh]

brooch una spilla [sp*eel*-lah]

brother: my brother mio fratello [m*ee*-oh . . .]

brown marrone [mar-r*oh*-nay]

brown paper la carta de pacchi [. . . p*ak*-kee]

browse: can I just browse around? posso curiosare? [. . . −s*ah*-ray]

bruise una ammaccatura

brunette una mora

brush *(noun)* una spazzola [sp*at*-tzo-lah] *(artist's)* un pennello

Brussels sprouts i cavolini di Bruxelles [. . . dee brook-se*l*]

bucket il secchio [s*ay*k-yoh]

buffet il buffet

building un edificio [ay-dee-*fee*-choh]

bump: he bumped his head ha urtato la testa [ah . . .]

bumper il paraurti [pa-ra-*oor*-tee]

bunk una cuccetta [koo-ch*ay*t-tah]

bunk beds i letti a castello

buoy una boa

burglar un ladro

burned: this meat is burned questa carne è bruciata [. . . k*a*r-nay eh broo-ch*ah*-tah]

my arms are burned mi sono scottato le braccia [. . . br*ah*-chah]

can you give me something for these burns? mi può dare qualcosa per queste scottature? [mee pwoh d*ah*-ray . . . skot-ta-*too*-ray]

bus l'autobus [*ow*-toh-boos]

bus stop la fermata dell'autobus

could you tell me when we get there? me lo può dire quando ci siamo? [may loh pwoh d*ee*-ray kw*a*n-doh chee see-*ah*-moh]

» *TRAVEL TIP: get tickets from machine on the bus; or buy a book of tickets from newsstand or tobacconist; usually flat fare; in Rome and Milan subway tickets valid for bus travel up to 1 hour from issue*

business: I'm here on business sono qui per affari [. . . kwee payr . . .]

business trip un viaggio d'affari [vee-*ah*-joh . . .]

none of your business non è affar suo [. . . eh . . .]

bust il busto [b*oo*s-toh]

» *TRAVEL TIP: bust measurements*

US	32	34	36	38	40
Italy	80	87	91	97	102

busy occupato

but ma
  not this one but that one non questo ma
  quello
butcher il macellaio [ma-chel-lah-yoh]
butter il burro [boor-roh]
button un bottone [bot-toh-nay]
buy: where can I buy...? dove posso comprare
  [doh-vay ... kom-prah-ray]
  I'll buy it lo compro
by: I'm here by myself sono qui [kwee] da solo
  are you by yourself? è qui da solo? [eh ...]
  can you do it by tomorrow? può farlo per
  domani? [pwoh ... payr ...]
  by train/car/plane in treno/auto/aereo [een
  treh-noh/ow-toh/ah-eh-ray-oh]
  I parked by the trees no parcheggiato vicino
  agli alberi [o par-kay-jah-toh vee-chee-noh al-
  yee al-bay-ree]
  who's it made by? chi l'ha fatto? [kee lah ...]
c *(on faucet)* hot
cabaret il cabaret
cabbage un cavolo [kah-vo-loh]
cable il cavo [kah-voh]
  cable car la funivia [−vee-ah]
cabin *(on ship)* una cabina
caduta massi *falling rocks*
cafe un caffè [kaf-feh]
» *TRAVEL TIP: Italian cafes also serve alcoholic
  drinks, but only snacks—toasted sandwiches
  and cakes; for cafe-type food look for the sign
  "tavola calda"*
cake una pasta
  a piece of cake un pezzo di torta [pet-tzoh
  dee ...]
calculator un calcolatore [−toh-ray]
call: will you call the manager? mi chiama il
  direttore? [mee kee-ah-mah eel
  dee-rayt-toh-ray]
  what is this called? come si [see] chiama?
calm calmo
  calm down si calmi [see ...]

camera la macchina fotografica [mak-kee-nah . . .]
camp: is there somewhere we can camp? dove possiamo accamparci? [doh-vay . . . ak-kam-par-chee]
  can we camp here? possiamo accamparci qua?
  camping trip una vacanza compeggio [va-kan-tzah kam-pay-joh]
  campsite un camping
» *TRAVEL TIP: in Italy you can camp almost anywhere; the best campsites are those recommended by ENIT (the national tourist organization)*
can *(tin)* un barattolo [ba-rat-toh-loh]
can¹: a can of beer una lattina di birra [. . . dee beer-rah]
  can-opener un apriscatole [a-pree-skah-toh-lay]
can²: can I have . . . ? posso avere . . . ? [. . . a-vay-ray]
  can you show me . . . ? può mostrarmi . . . ? [pwoh . . . –mee]
  I can't . . . non posso . . .
  he can't . . . non può . . .
  can we . . . ? possiamo . . . ?
Canada il Canada
Canadian canadese [ka-na-day-say]
cancel: I want to cancel my reservation vorrei cancellare la mia prenotazione [vor-ray-kan-chel-lah-ray lah mee-ah pray-no-ta-tzee-oh-nay]
  can we cancel dinner for tonight? possiamo cancellare la cena per stasera? [. . . chay-nah . . . sta-say-rah]
candle una candela [–day-lah]
  by candlelight al lume de candela [loo-may dee . . .]
cane il bastone da passeggio [bas-toh-nay . . .]
capsize capovolgersi [ka-po-vol-jer-see]
car l'auto [ow-toh], la macchina [mak-kee-nah]
  by car in macchina

....

carafe una caraffa
carbonated gassato
carburetor il carburatore [−*toh*-ray]
cards le carte [k*ar*-tay]
  do you play cards? gioca a carte?
  [jo-kah . . .]
care: will you take care of this for me? può
  prendersi cura di questo per me? [pwoh
  pren-der-see koo-rah dee kw*es*-toh payr may]
careful: be careful sta attento
car-ferry il traghetto [tra-gh*et*-toh]
carpet il tappeto *(wall-to-wall)* la moquette
  [−k*et*]
carrot la carota
carry: will you carry this for me? mi può
  portare questo? [mee pwoh por-t*ah*-ray . . .]
carving un intaglio [een-t*al*-yoh]
case *(suitcase)* una valigia [va-l*ee*-jah]
casello a . . .   *freeway toll at . . .*
cash *(money)* soldi [sol-dee]
  I haven't any cash non l'ho di moneta [. . . lo
  dee mo-n*ay*-tah]
  cash register la cassa
  will you cash a check for me? può
  riscuotere un assegno per me? [pwoh
  rees-kw*oh*-tay-ray oon as-s*ay*n-yoh payr may]
casino il casinò [ka-see-n*oh*]
» *TRAVEL TIP: it is important to stress the last*
  syllable; pronounced as in English the word
  means brothel
cassa   *cash register; cashier*
cassette una cassetta
castle il castello
cat il gatto
catch: where do we catch the bus? dove si
  prende l'autobus? [d*oh*-vay see pren-day
  low-toh-boos]
  he's caught a bug si è preso un malanno [see
  eh pr*ay*-soh . . .]
cathedral la cattedrale [−dr*ah*-lay]

catholic cattolico [kat-*toh*-lee-koh]
cauliflower il cavolfiore [−*oh*-ray]
cave la grotta
ceiling il soffitto
celery il sedano [*seh*-da-noh]
centigrade centigradi [chen-*tee*-gra-dee]
» *TRAVEL TIP: to convert C to F:* $\frac{C}{5} \times 9 + 32 = F$

centigrade −5 0 10 15 21 30 36.9
Fahrenheit 23 32 50 59 70 86 98.4
centimeter un centimetro [chen-*tee*-may-troh]
» *TRAVEL TIP: 1 cm = 0.39 inches*
center il centro [chen-troh]
  how do we get to the center? come si va in
  centro? [k*oh*-may see . . .]
central centrale [chen-tr*ah*-lay]
  with central heating con riscaldamento
  centrale
certain certo [ch*ay*r-troh]
  are you certain? è certo? [eh . . .]
certificate il certificato [cher-tee-fee-k*ah*-toh]
chain la catena [ka-t*ay*-nah]
chair la sedia [*seh*-dee-ah]
chairlift la seggiovia [seh-jo-v*ee*-ah]
champagne lo champagne [shom-p*an*-yuh]
change: could you change this into lire? può
  cambiare questi in lire? [pwoh kam-bee-
  ah-ray . . .]
  I don't have any change non ho moneta
  [. . . o mo-n*ay*-tah]
  do we have to change trains? dobbiamo
  cambiare treno?
  I'll just get changed vado a cambiarmi
» *TRAVEL TIP: don't be surprised if instead of
  small change you get chewing gum or candy
  when shopping or in a bar!*
» *TRAVEL TIP: changing money: as well as banks
  look for "Agenzia di Cambio"*
channel: the Channel la Manica [m*ah*-
  nee-kah]

....

charge: what do you charge? quanto fate
pagare? [. . . f*ah*-tay pa-g*ah*-ray]
  who's in charge? chi è l'incaricato? [kee
  eh . . .]
chart la carta
cheap a buon mercato [ah bwon mayr-k*ah*-toh]
  something cheaper qualcosa di meno caro
  [. . . dee m*ay*-noh . . .]
cheat: I've been cheated sono stato imbrogliato
  [. . . st*ah*-toh eem-brol-y*ah*-toh]
check *(noun)* un assegno [as-s*ay*n-yoh]
  will you take a check? prende un assegno?
  [pren-day . . .]
  checkbook il libretto di assegni
  [. . . dee . . .]
check: will you check? può controllare?
  [pwoh . . . –*ah*-ray]
  I'm sure, I've checked sono sicuro, ho
  controllato [. . . o . . .]
  will you check the total? può controllare il
  totale [. . . –l*ay*]
  we checked in ci siamo registrati [chee . . .]
  we checked out abbiamo pagato il conto
cheek la guancia [gwan-chah]
cheers salute [–tay] *(thank you)* grazie
  [gr*ah*-tzee-ay]
cheese il formaggio [for-m*ah*-joh]
chest il petto [pet-toh]
» *TRAVEL TIP: chest measurements*

US	34	36	38	40	42	44	46
Italy	87	91	97	102	107	112	117

chicken il pollo
chickenpox la varicella [va-ree-ch*el*-lah]
child il bambino [bam-b*ee*-noh]
  children i bambini [ee bam-b*ee*-nee]
  children's portion una porzione per bambini
  [. . . por-tzee-*oh*-nay . . .]
chin il mento
china la porcellana [por-chel-l*ah*-nah]
chips *(casino)* le fiches [lay feesh]
chiuso closed

chocolate il cioccolato [chok-ko-*lah*-toh]
  hot chocolate la cioccolata calda
  a box of chocolates una scatola di
  cioccolatini [s*kah*-toh-lah dee . . .]
choke *(car)* la valvola dell'aria [*val*-vo-lah
  del-*lah*-ree-ah]
chop *(noun)* una cotoletta
Christmas Natale [ne-*tah*-lay]
  Merry Christmas! buon Natale! [bwon . . .]
church la chiesa [kee-*ay*-sah]
  **where is the Protestant/Catholic
  church?** dov'è la chiesa protestante/cattolica?
  [doh-v*eh* . . . pro-tes-*tan*-tay/kat-*toh*-lee-kah]
cider il sidro [*see*-droh]
cigar il sigaro [*see*-ga-roh]
cigarette una sigaretta
  would you like a cigarette? vuole una
  sigaretta? [vw*oh*-lay . . .]
circle il circolo [ch*ee*r-ko-loh]
city la città [cheet-t*ah*]
claim *(noun: insurance)* la domanda
  d'indennizzo [. . . deen-den-n*ee*t-tzoh]
clarify chiarire [kee-a-*ree*-ray]
clean *(adjective)* pulito [poo-l*ee*-toh]
  can I have some clean sheets? posso avere
  le lenzuola pulite? [. . . a-v*ay*-ray lay
  layn-tzw*o*-lah . . .]
  my room hasn't been cleaned today la mia
  stanza non è stata pulita oggi [m*ee*-ah
  st*an*-tzah . . . eh . . . *o*-jee]
  it's not clean non è pulito
clear: I'm not clear about it non è chiaro
  [. . . eh kee-*ah*-roh]
clear up: do you think it'll clear up later?
  pensa che si rischiarerà più tardi? [. . . kay see
  rees-kee-a-ra-ray*rah* pew t*ar*-dee]
clever intelligente [−tay]
climate il clima [kl*ee*-mah]
climb: we're going to climb . . . andiamo a
  scalare . . . [. . . ska-l*ah*-ray]
  climber uno scalatore [−*toh*-ray]

clip *(skiing)* la pinzetta [peen-tz*ay*t-tah]

clock l'orologio [–*oh*-joh]

close¹ vicino [vee-ch*ee*-noh]

close²: when do you close? quando chiudete?
[. . . kee-oo-d*ay*-tay]

closed chiuso [kee-*oo*-soh]

cloth la stoffa *(rag)* uno straccio [str*ah*-choh]

clothes i vestiti [ee ves-*tee*-tee]

clothespin la molletta da bucato
[. . . boo-k*ah*-toh]

cloud la nuvola [n*oo*-vo-lah]

clutch la frizione [free-tzee-*oh*-nay]
   the clutch is slipping la frizione non si [see]
   innesta

coast la costa
   coast guard la guardia costiera [gw*ar*-dee-ah
   kos-tee-*eh*-rah]

coat il cappotto

coatroom il guardaroba [gw*ar*-da-r*o*-bah]

cockroach uno scarafaggio [–f*adj*-yoh]

coffee un caffè [kaf-f*eh*]
   coffee with milk un cappuccino
   [kap-poo-ch*ee*-noh]

» *TRAVEL TIP: in Italy coffee is always served
   black and very strong; if you want it less strong
   ask for "un caffè lungo"*

coin una moneta [mo-n*ay*-tah]

cold *(adjective)* freddo
   I'm cold ho freddo [o . . .]
   I've got a cold ho il raffreddore
   [. . . –d*oh*-ray]

collapse: he's collapsed ha avuto un collasso
   [ah . . .]

collar il colletto
   collarbone l'osso del collo

» *TRAVEL TIP: collar sizes*

US	14	14½	15	15½	16	16½	17
continental	36	37	38	39	41	42	43

collect: I want to collect . . . sono venuto a
   prendere . . . [. . . pren-d*ay*-ray]

collect call: I want to make a collect call to New York vorrei fare una chiamata a Nuova York a carico del destinatario [vor-*ray* f*ah*-ray *oo*-nah kee-a-m*ah*-tah . . .]

color un colore [ko-l*oh*-ray]
  have you any other colors? avete altri colori? [a-v*ay*-tay . . .]

comb il pettine [p*et*-tee-nay]

come venire [vay-n*ee*-ray]
  I come from New York sono di Nuova York [. . . dee noo-*oh*-vah . . .]
  we came here yesterday siamo arrivati ieri [. . . y*eh*-ree]
  come on! andiamo!
  come with me venga con me [. . . may]
  come here venga qui [. . . kwee]

comfortable comodo [k*o*-mo-doh]
  it's not very comfortable non è molto comodo

Common Market il Mercato Comune [mayr-k*ah*-toh ko-m*oo*-nay]

company la compagnia [kom-pan-y*ee*-ah]
  you're good company sei simpatico [say seem-p*ah*-tee-koh]

compartment *(train)* uno scompartimento

compass la bussola [b*oos*-so-lah]

compensation un compenso
  I demand compensation voglio un compenso [v*ol*-yoh . . .]

complaint una lamentela
  I want to complain about my room vorrei sporgere una lamentela a proposito della mia stanza [vor-r*ay* sp*or*-jay-ray . . . m*ee*-ah st*an*-tzah]

completely completamente [–m*ay*n-tay]

complicated: it's very complicated è molto complicato [eh . . .]

compliment: my compliments to the chef i miei complimenti allo chef [ee mee-*eh*-ee . . .]

concert un concerto [kon-ch*ay*r-toh]

concussion la commozione cerebrale
   [. . . -tzee-*oh*-nay chay-ray-br*ah*-lay]
condition la condizione [−tzee-*oh*-nay]
   it's not in very good condition non è in
   buone condizioni [. . . eh een bw*o*-nay . . .]
condom un preservat*ivo*
conference una conferenza [−*en*-tzah]
confirm confermare [kon-fayr-m*ah*-ray]
confuse: you're confusing me mi confonde
   [mee kon-f*on*-day]
congratulations! complimenti! [−*tee*]
conjunctivitis la congiuntivite
   [kon-joon-tee-v*ee*-tay]
connection *(rail, etc.)* la coincidenza
   [ko-een-chee-d*en*-tzah]
connoisseur un conoscitore [ko-no-shee-t*oh*-ray]
conscious conscio [kon-shoh]
consciousness: he's lost consciousness è
   svenuto [eh . . .]
constipation la stitichezza [stee-tee-k*ayt*-tzah]
consul il console [kon-so-lay]
consulate il consolato
contact: how can I contact . . . ? come mi metto
   in contatto con . . . ? [k*oh*-may mee . . .]
   contact lenses le lenti a contatto
contraceptive un contraccettivo
   [kon-tra-chet-t*ee*-voh]
convenient conveniente [−*en*-tay]
cook: it's not cooked è crudo
   it's beautifully cooked è cucinato alla
   perfezione [eh koo-chee-n*ah*-toh *a*l-lah
   per-fay-tzee-*oh*-nay]
cookie il biscotto
cool fresco
corkscrew un cavatappi
corn *(foot)* un callo
corner un angolo [*an*-go-loh]
   can we have a corner table? possiamo avere
   un tavolo d'angolo [. . . a-v*ay*-ray oon
   t*ah*-vo-loh . . .]
cornflakes i [ee] corn flakes

correct corretto
cosmetics i cosmetici [ee kos-m*eh*-tee-chee]
cost: what does it cost? quanto costa?
   that's too much è troppo
   I'll take it lo compro
cotton il cotone [ko-t*oh*-nay]
cough la tosse [tos-say]
   cough drops le pastiglie per la tosse
   [pas-t*eel*-yay . . .]
could: could you please . . . ? potrebbe . . . ?
   [po-tr*ay*b-bay)
   could I have . . . ? potrei avere . . . ?
   [po-tr*ay* a-v*ay*-ray]
country un paese [pa-*ay*-say]
   in the country in campagna [een
   kam-p*a*n-yah]
couple: a couple of . . . un paio di . . . [p*ah*-yoh
   dee]
courier la guida [gw*ee*-dah]
course *(of meal)* una portata
   of course certo [ch*ay*r-toh]
court: I'll take you to court la cito in tribunale
   [lah ch*ee*-toh een tree-boo-n*ah*-lay]
cousin un cugino [koo-j*ee*-noh]
cover: keep him well covered lo tenga ben
   coperto; **cover charge** il coperto
cow la mucca [m*oo*k-kah]
crab il granchio [gr*a*n-kee-oh]
crash: there's been a crash c'è stato uno
   scontro [cheh st*ah*-toh . . .]
   crash helmet un casco
crazy: you're crazy è pazzo [eh p*a*t-tzoh]
cream la crema *(fresh)* la panna
crèche l'asilo nido [a-s*ee*-loh n*ee*-doh]
credit card una carta di credito [. . . dee
   kr*eh*-dee-toh]
crisis una crisi [kr*ee*-see]
crossroads l'incrocio [een-kr*oh*-choh]
crowded affollato
cruise una crociera [kro-ch*ay*-rah]
crutch una gruccia [gr*oo*-chah]

cry: don't cry non piangere [non pee-*a*n-jay-ray]
cup una tazza [t*a*t-tzah]
   a cup of coffee una tazza di caffè [. . . dee kaf-f*e*h]
cupboard un armadio [ar-m*ah*-dee-oh]
curry il curry
curtains le tende [t*e*n-day]
cushion il cuscino [koo-sh*ee*-noh]
Customs la Dogana
cut: I've cut myself mi sono tagliato [mee-s*o*h-noh tal-y*ah*-toh]
cycle: can we cycle there? ci si può andare con la bicicletta? [chee see pwoh an-d*ah*-ray kon la bee-chee-kl*ay*t-tah]
cyclist un ciclista [chee-kl*ee*s-tah]
cylinder il cilindro [chee-l*ee*n-droh]
   cylinder head gasket la guarnizione del cilindro [gwar-nee-tzee-*oh*-nay . . .]
dad(dy) il papà
damage: I'll pay for the damage pago per il guasto [gw*a*s-toh]
   it's damaged è danneggiato [eh dan-nay-j*ah*-toh]
damn! maledizione! [ma-lay-dee-tzee-*oh*-nay]
damp umido [*oo*-mee-doh]
dance: is there a dance on? si balla? [see . . .]
   would you like to dance? vuoi ballare? [vwo-ee bal-l*ah*-ray]
dangerous pericoloso
dark scuro
   when does it get dark? quando fa buio? [. . . b*oo*-yoh]
   dark green verde scuro [v*ay*r-day . . .]
darling tesoro
dashboard il cruscotto
date: what's the date? quanti ne [nay] abbiamo?
   can we fix a date? possiamo fissare un appuntamento? [. . . fees-s*ah*-ray . . .]
   on the first of March il primo marzo [pr*ee*-moh m*a*r-tzoh]

on the fifth of May il cinque maggio
[chee*n*-kway m*ah*-joh]
in 1982 nel millenovecentottantadue
[m*ee*l-lay-no-vay-che*n*-toh-ot-tan-ta-d*oo*-ay]
» TRAVEL TIP: *to say the date just use the ordinary*
number as shown above (the exception is "the
first"); numbers are listed on page 127
dates *(fruit)* i datteri [ee d*a*t-tay-ree]
daughter: my daughter mia figlia [m*ee*-ah
fee*l*-yah]
day il giorno [jor-noh]
dead morto
deaf sordo
deal *(business)* un affare [af-*fah*-ray]
it's a deal affare fatto
will you deal with it? se ne occupa lei? [say
nay *o*k-koo-pah lay]
dear: Dear Sir Egregio Signore [ay-gr*ay*-joh
seen-*yoh*-ray]
Dear Madam Egregia Signora
Dear Franco Caro Franco
December dicembre [dee-ch*em*-bray]
deck il ponte [pon-tay]
deckchair una sedia a sdraio [s*eh*-dee-ah ah
sdr*ah*-yoh]
declare: I have nothing to declare non ho
niente da dichiarare [non o nee-*en*-tay dah
deek-ya-r*ah*-ray]
deep profondo
is it deep? è profondo? [eh . . .]
defendant l'accusato
delay: the flight was delayed il volo ha avuto
un ritardo [. . . ah a-v*oo*-toh . . .]
deliberately apposta
delicate *(person)* delicato
delicatessen una salumeria [−may-r*ee*-ah]
delicious delizioso [day-lee-tzee-*oh*-soh]
delivery: is there another mail delivery? c'è
un'altra distribuzione di posta? [cheh . . .
−tzee-*oh*-nay dee p*o*s-tah]
deluxe di lusso [dee l*oo*s-soh]

democratic democratico [day-mo-kr*ah*-tee-koh]

dent una ammaccatura
you've dented my car ha ammaccato la mia
auto [ah ... m*ee*-ah *ow*-toh]

dentist il dentista
YOU MAY THEN HEAR...
apra bene *open wide*
si sciacqui *please rinse out*

dentures la dentiera [dent-y*ah*-rah]

deny: I deny it lo nego

deodorant il deodorante [−tay]

departure la partenza [par-t*en*-tzah]

depend: it depends (on him) dipende (da lui)
[dee-pen-day dah l*oo*-ee]

deport deportare [−t*ah*-ray]

deposit un deposito [day-po-see-toh]
do I have to leave a deposit? devo lasciare
un deposito? [d*ay*-voh la-sh*ah*-ray ...]

deposito bagagli *left luggage*

depressed depresso

depth la profondità [pro-fon-dee-t*ah*]

desperate: I'm desperate for a drink ho una
sete terribile [o *oo*-nah s*ay*-tay ter-r*ee*-bee-lay]

dessert il dolce [d*ol*-chay]

destination la destinazione [−tzee-*oh*-nay]

detergent il detergente [−jen-tay]

detour una deviazione [−tzee-*oh*-nay]

devalued svalutato

develop: could you develop these? può
sviluppare questi? [pwoh svee-loop-
p*ah*-ray ...]

deviazione *diversion*

diabetic un diabetico [dee-a-b*eh*-tee-koh]

dialing code il prefisso

diamond un diamante [−tay]

diaper il pannolino [pah-no-l*ee*-noh]

diarrhea la diarrea [dee-ar-r*ay*-ah]
have you got something for diarrhea? ha
qualcosa per la diarrea? [ah ...]

diary il diario [dee-*ah*-ree-oh]

dictionary il dizionario [dee-tzee-o-n*ah*-ree-oh]

didn't *see* **not**
die morire [mo-r*ee*-ray]
  he's dying sta morendo
diesel *(fuel)* il diesel
diet la dieta [dee-*ay*-tah]
  I'm on a diet sono a dieta
different: they are different sono diversi
  can I have a different room? posso avere
  un'altra camera? [. . . a-v*ay*-ray . . .]
  is there a different route? c'è un altra
  strada? [chen . . .]
difficult difficile [deef-f*ee*-chee-lay]
digestion la digestione [−*oh*-nay]
dinghy il dinghy
dining room la sala da pranzo [. . . pr*an*-tzoh]
dinner la cena [ch*ay*-nah]
  dinner jacket lo smoking
direct *(adjective)* diretto [dee−]
  does it go direct? ci va diretto? [chee . . .]
dirty sporco
disabled invalido [een-v*ah*-lee-doh]
disappear sparire [spa-r*ee*-ray]
  it's just disappeared è sparito [eh . . .]
disappointing deludente [−tay]
disco la discoteca
  see you in the disco ci vediamo in discoteca
  [chee . . .]
discount lo sconto
disgusting disgustoso
dish un piatto [pee-*at*-toh]
dishonest disonesto
disinfectant un disinfettante [−tay], l'alcole
» *TRAVEL TIP: the latter, which is pure alcohol,*
  usually pink in color, is the standard
  disinfectant
distance: in the distance in lontananza [een
  lon-ta-n*an*-tzah]
distress signal un segnale di soccorso
  [sayn-y*ah*-lay dee . . .]
distributor *(car)* lo spinterogeno
  [speen-tay-r*o*-jay-noh]

disturb: the noise is disturbing me il rumore
mi disturba [eel roo-m*oh*-ray mee dees-
toor-bah]

divieto di . . . *do not* . . .

divorced divorziato [dee-vor-tzee-*ah*-toh]

do: how do you do? piacere [pee-a-ch*ay*-ray]

   what are you doing tonight? cosa fa
stasera?

   how do you do it? come fa? [k*oh*-may fah]

   will you do it for me? lo può fare lei? [loh
pwoh f*ah*-ray lay]

   I've never done it before non l'ho mai fatto
prima [non lo m*ah*-ee f*a*t-toh pr*ee*-mah]

   I was doing 60 kph andavo a sessanta all'ora

doctor il medico [m*eh*-dee-koh]

   I need a doctor ho bisogno di un medico
[o bee-sonn-yoh dee . . .]

» *TRAVEL TIP: any pharmacy (farmacia) will have
a list of the nearest doctors*
YOU MAY THEN HEAR . . .
l'è mai successo prima? *have you had this
before?*
dove le fa male? *where does it hurt?*
sta prendendo delle medicine? *are you taking
any drugs?*
ne prenda una/due . . . *take one/two* . . .
una volta/due volte/tre volte al giorno
once/twice/three times a day

document il documento

dog il cane [k*ah*-nay]

dogana *customs*

don't! no!; *see* not

door la porta

dosage la dose [d*oh*-say]

double: double room una camera a due letti
[k*ah*-may-rah ah d*oo*-ay let-teeh]
(with double bed) una camera matrimoniale
[−ee-*ah*-lay]

   double whisky un whisky doppio
[. . . d*o*p-pee-oh]

down: get down! giù! [joo]
   downstairs dabbasso
   it's just down the road è qui vicino [eh kwee
   vee-ch*ee*-noh]
dozen una dozzina
drain il tubo di scarico [*too*-boh dee
   sk*ah*-ree-koh]
dress un vestito [ves-*tee*-toh]
» *TRAVEL TIP: sizes*

US	5	7	9	11	12	13	14
Italy	38	38	40	40	42	42	44

dressing *(for wound)* la medicazione
   (may-dee-ka-tzee-*oh*-nay)
   (for salad) il condimento
**drink: would you like something to
   drink?** vuole bere qualcosa? [vw*oh*-lay
   b*ay*-ray . . .]
   I don't drink non bevo alcolici [. . . b*ay*-voh
   al-k*oh*-lee-chee]
   I had too much to drink ho [o] bevuto troppo
   is the water drinkable? l'acqua è potabile?
   [. . . eh po-t*ah*-bee-lay]
drive guidare [gwee-d*ah*-ray]
   I've been driving all day è tutto il giorno
   che guido [eh t*oot*-toh eel j*or*-noh kay . . .]
driver l'autista [low-t*ee*s-tah]
driving license la patente [pa-ten-tay]
drown: he's drowning sta annegando
drug la droga
drugstore la farmacia [far-ma-ch*ee*-ah]
drunk unbriaco [oo-bree-*ah*-koh]
dry *(adjective)* asciutto [a-sh*oot*-toh]
   (wine) secco
   dry cleaner's un lavasecco
due: when is the bus due? quando arriva
   l'autobus? [. . . l*ow*-toh-boos]
during durante [doo-r*an*-tay]
dust la polvere [p*ol*-vay-ray]
duty-free *(noun)* il duty-free
dynamo la dinamo [d*ee*-na-moh]

each: can we have one each? possiamo averne
uno ciascuno [. . . a-v*ay*r-nay *oo*-noh
chas-k*oo*-noh]
   how much are they each? quanto costano
l'uno?
ear l'orecchio [or-r*ay*k-yoh]
   I have an earache ho il mal d'orecchi [o . . .]
early presto
   we want to leave a day earlier vogliamo
partire un giorno prima [vol-y*ah*-moh par-t*ee*-
ray oon jor-noh pr*ee*-mah]
   early closing la chiusura anticipata
[kee-oo-s*oo*-rah an-tee-chee-p*ah*-tah]
earring l'orecchino [o-r*ay*k-k*ee*-noh]
east est
Easter Pasqua [p*as*-kwah]
easy facile [f*ah*-chee-lay]
eat mangiare [man-j*ah*-ray]
   something to eat qualcosa da mangiare
egg un uovo [w*o*-voh]
eggplant la melanzana [may-lan-tz*ah*-nah]
either: either . . . or . . . o . . . o . . .
   I don't like either non mi piace nessuno dei
due [non mee pee-*ah*-chay nes-s*oo*-noh day
d*oo*-ay]
elastic elastico [ay-l*as*-tee-koh]
elbow il gomito [g*o*-mee-toh]
electric elettrico [ay-l*et*-tree-koh]
   electric blanket la coperta elettrica
   electric heater la stufetta elettrica
electrical outlet la presa (di corrente) [pr*ay*-sah
dee kor-r*en*-tay]
electrician l'elettricista [ay-layt-tree-ch*ees*-tah]
electricity l'elettricità [ay-layt-tree-chee-t*ah*]
elegant elegante [. . . –tay]
elevator l'ascensore
   the elevator isn't working l'ascensore non
funziona [la-shayn-s*oh*-ray non
foon-tzee-*oh*-nah]
else: something else qualcosa d'altro

somewhere else da qualche altra parte
[dah-kwal-kay al-trah par-tay]
who else? chi altro? [kee . . .]
or else o altrimenti
embarrassed imbarazzato [eem-ba-rat-tzah-toh]
embarrassing imbarazzante
[eem-ba-rat-tzan-tay]
embassy l'ambasciata [am-ba-shah-tah]
emergency emergenza [ay-mayr-jen-tzah]
empty vuoto [vwo-toh]
enclose: I enclose . . . accludo . . .
end la fine [fee-nay]
when does it end? quando finisce . . . ?
[. . . fee-nee-shay]
engaged *(person)* fidanzato [fee-dan-tzah-toh]
engagement ring anello de fidanzamento
[. . . dee fee-dan-tza-men-toh]
engine il motore (mo-toh-ray)
engine trouble un guasto al motore
[gwas-toh . . .]
England l'Inghilterra [een-gheel-ter-rah]
English inglese [een-glay-say]
the English gli Inglesi [lee . . .]
do you speak English? parla l'inglese?
enjoy: I enjoyed it very much mi è piaciuto
molto [mee eh pee-a-choo-toh mol-toh]
enlargement *(photo)* un ingrandimento
enormous enorme [ay-nor-may]
enough: thank you, that's enough basta,
grazie [. . . grah-tzee-ay]
entertainment il divertimento [dee-vayr-tee−]
entrance l'entrata
entrata entrance
entry l'entrata
envelope una busta [boos-tah]
equipment l'equipaggiamento
[ay-kwee-pa-ja-men-toh]
error un errore [ayr-roh-ray]
escalator la scala mobile [. . . mo-bee-lay]
especially specialmente [spay-chal-men-tay]

essential essenziale [es-sen-tzee-*ah*-lay]
  it is essential that... è indispensabile
  che... [eh een-dees-pen-s*ah*-bee-lay kay]
evacuate evacuare [−ray]
even: even the Americans perfino gli
  Americani [per-*fee*-noh lee ...]
evening la sera [s*ay*-rah]
  this evening stasera
  in the evening la sera
  good evening buona sera [bwo-nah...]
  evening dress l'abito da sera [*ah*-bee-toh...]
ever: have you ever been to...? è mai stato
  a...? [eh m*ah*-ee...]
every ogni [on-yee]
  every day ogni giorno [...jor-noh]
everyone tutti [*toot*-tee]
  everything tutto
  everywhere dappertutto
exact esatto
example esempio [ay-*sem*-pee-oh]
  for example per esempio
excellent eccellente [ay-chayl-*len*-tay]
except: except me eccetto me [ay-ch*et*-toh may]
excess eccesso [ay-ch*es*-soh]
  excess baggage bagaglio eccedente
  [ba-g*al*-yoh ay-chay-d*en*-tay]
exchange *(money)* cambio [k*am*-bee-oh]
exciting entusiasmante [−ray]
  how exciting! che bello! [kay...]
excursion una gita [j*ee*-tah]
excuse me *(to get past)* permesso
  (to get attention) scusi [sko*o*-zee]
  (apology) mi scusi [mee...]
exhaust *(car)* lo scappamento
exhausted sfinito [sfee-n*ee*-toh]
exhibition un'esposizione [ays-po-see-tzee-*oh*-nay]
exhibitor un espositore [−ray]
exit l'uscita [oo-sh*ee*-tah]
expect: she's expecting è incinta [eh
  een-ch*ee*n-tah]

expenses: it's on an expense account è a spese della ditta [eh ah sp*ay*-say d*e*l-lah d*eet*-tah]

expensive costoso

expert esperto

explain spiegare [spee-ay-g*ah*-ray]
would you explain that slowly? può spiegarlo lentamente? [pwoh spee-ay-g*a*r-loh len-ta-m*e*n-tay]

export *(noun)* l'esportazione [ays-por-ta-tzee-*oh*-nay]

express espresso

extra *(adjective):* **an extra day** un altro giorno
is that extra? è extra? [eh . . .]

extremely estremamente [−tay]

eye l'occhio [ok-yoh]
eyebrow il sopracciglio [so-pra-ch*ee*l-yoh]
eyeshadow l'ombretto

eyewitness un testimone oculare [tes-tee-m*oh*-nay o-koo-l*ah*-ray]

F (on faucet) cold

face la faccia [f*ah*-chah]
face mask *(diving)* la maschera [m*as*-kay-rah]

fact il fatto

factory la fabbrica [f*a*b-bree-kah]

Fahrenheit il Fahrenheit

» *TRAVEL TIP: to convert F to C:* $F - 32 \times \frac{5}{9} = C$

Fahrenheit	23	32	50	59	70	86	98.4
centigrade	−5	0	10	15	21	30	36.9

faint: she's fainted è svenuta [eh . . .]

fair una fiera [fee-*ay*-rah]
that's not fair non è giusto [. . . eh j*oo*s-toh]

faithfully: yours faithfully distinti saluti

fake falso

fall: he's fallen è caduto [eh . . .]

false falso
false teeth i denti finti [d*e*n-tee f*ee*ɲ-tee]

family la famiglia [fa-m*ee*l-yah]

....

fan il ventilatore [ven-tee-la-*toh*-ray]
  (hand-held) un ventaglio [ven-t*a*l-yoh]
  (football, etc.) un tifoso [tee−]
  fan-belt la cinghia [ch*ee*n-ghee-ah]
far lontano
  is it far? è lontano? [eh . . .]
  how far is it? quanto dista? [. . . dees-t*ah*]
fare *(travel)* (il prezzo del) biglietto [pr*e*t-tzoh
  dayl beel-y*e*t-toh]
farm la fattoria [fat-toh-r*ee*-ah]
farther più lontano [pew . . .]
fashion la moda
fast veloce [vay-l*o*h-chey]
  don't speak so fast non parli così in fretta
  [. . . ko-s*ee* . . .]
fat grasso
fatally fatalmente [−tay]
father: my father mio padre [m*ee*-oh p*a*h-dray]
fathom un braccio [br*a*h-choh]
faucet il rubinetto [roo-bee-n*a*yt-toh]
fault un difetto
  it's not my fault non è colpa mia [. . . m*ee*-ah]
faulty difettoso
favorite favorito [fa-vo-r*ee*-toh]
February febbraio [feb-br*a*h-yoh]
fed up: I'm fed up sono stufo [. . . st*oo*-foh]
feel: I feel cold/hot ho freddo/caldo [o . . .]
  I feel sad sono triste [. . . tr*ee*s-tay]
  I feel like . . . ho voglia di . . . [o v*o*l-yah dee]
ferry il traghetto [tra-g*a*yt-toh]
fever la febbre [f*e*b-bray]
  he's got a fever ha la febbre [ah lah f*e*b-bray]
few: only a few solo pochi [p*o*-kee]
  a few days pochi giorni [p*o*-kee j*o*r-nee]
fiancé(e) fidanzato (fidanzata)
  [fee-dan-tz*a*h-toh . . .]
field un campo
figs i fichi [ee f*ee*-kee]
figure *(number)* una cifra [ch*ee*-frah]
  I'm watching my figure sto attenta alla
  linea [. . . l*ee*-nay-ah]

fill: fill her up mi faccia il pieno [mee f*ah*-chah
eel pee-*eh*-noh]
   to fill in a form riempire un modulo
[ree-aym-p*ee*-ray oon m*o*-doo-loh]
fillet il filetto
film *(movie)* un film [feelm]
   do you have this type of film? avete questo
tipo di pellicola? [a-v*ay*-tay kwes-toh t*ee*-poh
dee payl-l*ee*-ko-lah]
filter un filtro
   filter/non-filter col filtro/senza filtro
find trovare [tro-v*ah*-ray]
   if you find it... se lo trova... [say...]
   I've found a... ho trovato un... [o...]
fine: fine weather bel tempo
   a 50,000 lire fine una multa di cinquanta
mila lire [m*oo*l-tah dee cheen-kw*a*n-tah
m*ee*-lah l*ee*-ray]
finger un dito [d*ee*-toh]
   fingernail l'unghia [*oo*n-ghee-ah]
finish: I haven't finished non ho finito [non o
fee-n*ee*-toh]
fire: fire! al fuoco! [fw*o*-koh]
   can we light a fire here? possiamo accendere
un fuoco qui? [...a-ch*e*n-day-ray oon fw*o*-koh
kwee]
   fire department i vigili del fuoco
[ee v*ee*-jee-lee del fw*o*-koh]
   fire extinguisher un estintore [ays-teen-
t*oh*-ray]
» *TRAVEL TIP: in the event of a fire phone 113*
first primo [pr*ee*-mo]
   I was first c'ero prima io [ch*eh*-roh pr*ee*-mah
ee-oh]
   first aid il pronto soccorso
   first aid kit la cassetta di [dee] pronto
soccorso
   first class di prima classe [dee pr*ee*-mah
kl*ah*-say]
   first name il nome di battesimo [n*oh*-may dee
bat-t*ay*-see-moh]

....

fish il pesce [p*ay*-shay]
fishing la pesca
  fishing rod la canna da pesca
five cinque [ch*ee*n-kway]
fix: can you fix it? *(repair)* può ripararlo?
  [pwoh ree-pa-r*ar*-loh]
flag la bandiera [ban-dee-*ay*-rah]
flash *(photo)* il flash
flat piatto [pee-*at*-toh]
  this drink is flat questa bibita è svanita
  [. . . b*ee*-bee-tah eh sva-n*ee*-tah]
  I've got a flat tire ho una foratura [o *oo*-nah
  fo-ra-t*oo*-ray]
flavor il sapore [sa-p*oh*-ray]
flea la pulce [p*oo*l-chay]
flight il volo
flippers le pinne [lay-p*ee*n-nay]
flirt *(verb)* flirtare [fleer-t*ah*-ray]
float *(verb)* galleggiare [gal-lay-j*ah*-ray]
floor il pavimento
  on the second floor al secondo piano
» *TRAVEL TIP: Europeans call the second floor the*
  first floor, the third floor the second floor, etc.
flower un fiore [fee-*oh*-ray]
  bunch of flowers un mazzo di fiori [m*at*-tzoh
  dee fee-*oh*-ree]
flu l'influenza [een-floo-*en*-tzah]
fly *(insect)* una mosca
  (trousers) la cerniera [chayr-nee-*ay*-rah]
foggy nebbioso
follow seguire [say-gw*ee*-ray]
food il cibo [ch*ee*-boh] *see pages 74–75*
  food poisoning avvelenamento da cibo
fool uno sciocco [sh*o*k-koh]
foot il piede [pee-*ay*-day]
» *TRAVEL TIP: 1 foot = 30.1 cm = 0.3 meters*
for per [payr]
forbidden vietato [vee-ay-t*ah*-toh]
foreign straniero [stran-y*eh*-roh]
  foreign exchange il cambio estero
  [k*am*-bee-oh *es*-tay-roh]

foreigner uno straniero [stran-*yeh*-roh]
forget dimenticare [dee-men-tee-k*ah*-ray]
  I forget, I've forgotten non mi ricordo
  don't forget non dimenticare
  I'll never forget you non ti dimenticherò mai
  [non tee dee-men-tee-kay-ro m*ah*-ee]
fork la forchetta [for-k*ay*t-tah]
form *(document)* un modulo [mo-doo-loh]
formal formale [for-m*ah*-lay]
fortnight due settimane [d*oo*-ay sayt-tee-
  m*ah*-nay]
forward *(adverb)* avanti
  could you forward my mail? può inoltrare la
  mia posta? [pwoh ee-nol-tr*ah*-ray la
  m*ee*-ah-pos-tah]
foundation *(makeup)* il fondotinta
fracture una frattura [frat-*too*-rah]
fragile fragile [fr*ah*-jee-lay]
France la Francia [fr*an*-chah]
free libero [*lee*-bay-roh]
  (no charge) gratis
  admission free ingresso libero
freeway l'autostrada [ow-toh-str*ah*-dah]
freight *(goods)* le merci [m*ay*r-chee]
French francese [fran-ch*ay*-say]
french fries le patatine fritte [lay pa-ta-*tee*-nay
  fr*ee*t-tay]
freshen up: I want to freshen up vorrei darmi
  una rinfrescata [vor-r*ay* d*ar*-mee . . .]
Friday venerdì [vay-nayr-d*ee*]
friend un amico [a-m*ee*-koh]
friendly cordiale [kor-dee-*ah*-lay]
from da
  where is it from? da dove viene? [dah d*oh*-vay
  vee-*ay*-nay]
front *(noun)* il davanti
  in front of you davanti a lei [. . . lay]
  at the front davanti
frost il gelo [j*ay*-loh]
  frostbite il congelamento [kon-jay-la-m*en*-toh]
frozen congelato [kon-jay-l*ah*-toh]

fruit la frutta
   fruit salad una macedonia [ma-chay-don-yah]
fry friggere [free-jay-ray]
   nothing fried niente di fritto [nee-en-tay dee free-toh]
   fried egg un uovo fritto [wo-voh . . .]
   frying pan una padella
fuel il combustibile [kom-boos-tee-bee-lay]
full pieno [pee-ay-noh]
fun: it's fun è divertente [eh dee-vayr-ten-tay]
funny *(comical)* buffo [boof-foh]
   (strange) strano [strah-noh]
furniture il mobilio [mo-beel-yoh]
further *(adverb)* oltre [ol-tray]
fuse un fusibile [foo-see-bee-lay]
future il futuro [foo-too-roh]
   in the future in futuro
gabinetti toilets
gale una bufera [boo-fay-rah]
galleria tunnel
gallon un gallone [−nay]
» *TRAVEL TIP: 1 gallon = 3.78 liters*
gallstone un calcolo [kal-ko-loh]
galoshes gli stivali di gomma [lee stee-vah-lee dee . . .]
gamble *(verb)* giocare d'azzardo [jo-kah-ray dat-tzar-doh]
garage il garage [ga-rah-jay]
» *TRAVEL TIP: Italian garages tend to close between 1:00 and 3:00 pm*
garbage la spazzatura [spat-tza-too-rah]
garden il giardino [jar-dee-noh]
garlic l'aglio [al-yoh]
gas il gasi; *(car)* la benzina [ben-tzee-nah]
   gas stove una cucina a gas [koo-chee-nah . . .]
   gas cylinder la bombola del gas [bom-bo-lah . . .]
   gas station il distributore di benzina [dees-tree-boo-toh-ray de . . .]
gasket la guarnizione [gwar-nee-tzee-oh-nay]

gay *(homosexual)* omosessuale
[o-mo-ses-soo-*ah*-lay]
gear la marcia [m*ar*-chah]
(equipment) l'attrezzatura [at-tray-tza-*too*-rah]
  gearbox la scatola del cambio [sk*ah*-toh-lah
del k*a*m-bee-oh]
  gearshift la leva del cambio [l*ay*-vah . . .]
  I can't get it into gear non riesco ad
innestare la marcia [non ree-*ay*s-koh ad
een-nes-t*ah*-ray . . .]
German tedesco
Germany la Germania [jayr-m*a*n-yah]
gesture un gesto [j*e*s-toh]
get: will you get me a . . . ? mi può prendere
un . . . ? [mee pwoh pr*e*n-day-ray oon . . .]
  how do I get to . . . ? come faccio per andare
a . . . ? [k*oh*-may f*ah*-choh payr an-d*ah*-ray
ah . . .]
  when can I get it back? quando me [may] lo
ritorna?
  where do I get off? dove scendo? [d*oh*-vay
sh*e*n-doh]
  when do we get back? quando torniamo?
  where can I get a bus for . . . ? dove posso
prendere un autobus per . . . ?
  will you come and get me? mi viene a
prendere? [mee vee-*ay*-nay ah pr*e*n-day-ray]
  have you got . . . ? ha . . . ? [ah]
gin il gin
  gin and tonic un gin and tonic
girl una ragazza [ra-g*a*t-tzah]
  my girlfriend la mia ragazza [m*e*-ah . . .]
give dare [d*ah*-ray]
  will you give me . . . ? mi dà . . . ? [mee . . .]
  I gave it to him gliel'ho dato [lee-*ay*-lo . . .]
glad contento
glass il vetro
  a glass un bicchiere [beek-y*e*h-ray]
glasses *(eye)* gli occhiali [ok-y*ah*-lee]
gloves i guanti [ee gw*a*n-tee]

....

glue la colla
go: my car won't go la mia macchina non parte
  [lah m*ee*-ah m*a*k-kee-nah non p*a*r-tay]
  when does the bus go? quando parte
  l'autobus? [kwan-doh p*a*r-tay l*o*w-toh-boos]
  where are you going? dove vai? [doh-vay
  vah-ee]
  the bus has gone l'autobus è partito
  he's gone è andato via [eh ... v*ee*-ah]
goat la capra
God il dio [d*ee*-oh]
goggles *(skiing)* gli occhiali da neve [lee
  ok-y*ah*-lee da n*a*y-vay]
gold l'oro
golf il golf
good buono [bw*o*-noh]
  good! bene! [b*a*y-nah]
good-bye arrivederci [ar-ree-vay-d*a*yr-chee], ciao
  [chow]
gooseberries uva spina [*oo*-vah sp*ee*-nah]
gram un grammo
» *TRAVEL TIP: 100 gram = approx. 3½ oz.*
grand grandioso [gran-dee-*oh*-soh]
  grandfather il nonno
  grandmother la nonna
  my grandson/granddaughter mio nipote/mia
  nipote [m*ee*-oh nee-p*oh*-tay/m*ee*-ah ...]
grapefruit il pompelmo
  grapefruit juice il succo di pompelmo
  [s*oo*k-koh dee]
grapes l'uva [*oo*-vah]
grass l'erba [*e*r-bah]
grateful grato [gr*ah*-toh]
  I'm very grateful to you le sono molto grato
  [lay ...]
gravy il sugo [s*oo*-goh]
gray grigio [gr*ee*-joh]
grease il grasso *(car, etc.)* il lubrificante
  [loo-bree-fee-k*a*n-tay]
greasy unto [*oo*n-toh]

great *(big)* grande [. . . day] *(very good)*
bellissimo
  great! benissimo!
greedy ingordo [een-gor-doh]
green verde [vayr-day]
  greengrocer's il fruttivendolo
  [froot-tee-ven-doh-loh]
grilled alla griglia [. . . greel-yah]
grocer una drogheria [dro-gay-ree-ah]
ground: on the ground a terra
  on the ground floor a pian terreno [ah
  pee-an tayr-rah-noh]
group un gruppo [groop-poh]
  our group leader il mostro capogruppo
  I'm with the English group sono con il
  gruppo degli Inglesi [dayl-yee een-glay-see]
guarantee: is there a guarantee? ha la
  garanzia? [ah lah ga-ran-tzee-ah]
guasto out of order
guest l'ospite [os-pee-tay]
guesthouse una pensione [payn-see-oh-nay]
guide una guida [gwee-dah]
guilty colpevole [kol-pay-vo-lay]
guitar una chitarra [kee-tar-rah]
gum *(chewing)* la gomma da masticare [−kah-ray]
gums *(in mouth)* le gengive [jen-jee-vay]
gun una pistola [pees-toh-lah]
gynecologist il ginecologo [jee-nay-ko-lo-goh]
hair i capelli *(plural)* [ee . . .]
  hairbrush una spazzola per capelli
  [spat-tzo-lah . . .]
  where can I get a haircut? dove posso farmi
  tagliare i capelli? [doh-vay pos-soh far-mee
  tal-yah-ray . . .]
  is there a hairdresser's here? c'è un
  parrucchiere qui? [cheh oon par-rook-yay-ray
  kwee]
half una metà [may-tah]
  a half portion una mezza porzione [met-tzah
  por-tzee-oh-nay]

half an hour mezz'ora
ham il prosciutto [pro-sh*oo*t-toh]
hamburger un hamburger
hammer un martello
hand la mano
  handbag la borsetta [bor-s*ay*t-tah]
  handbrake il freno a mano
handkerchief il fazzoletto [fat-tzoh-l*ay*t-toh]
handle *(door)* la maniglia [ma-n*eel*-yah]
  (cup) il manico [m*ah*-nee-koh]
hand luggage il bagaglio a mano
  [ba-g*al*-yoh . . .]
handmade lavorato a mano
handsome bello
hanger la gruccia [gr*oo*-chah]
hangover il mal di [dee] capo (dopo una
  sbornia)
  my head is killing me mi scoppia la testa
happen accadere [ak-ka-d*ay*-ray]
  I don't know how it happened non so come
  è successo [. . . k*oh*-may eh soo-ch*es*-soh]
  what's happening/happened? cosa succede/è
  successo? [. . . soo-ch*ay*-day . . .]
happy contento
harbor il porto
hard duro [d*oo*-roh]
  hard-boiled egg uovo sodo [w*o*-voh . . .]
  push hard spinga forte [sp*een*-gah for-t*ay*]
harm il male [m*ah*-lay]
hat il cappello
hate: I hate . . . odio . . . [o-dee-oh]
have avere [a-v*ay*-ray]
  I have a pain ho un dolore [o oon doh-l*oh*-ray]
  do you have any cigars/a map? ha dei
  sigari/una pianta? [ah day s*ee*-ga-ree . . .]
  can I have some water/some more? posso
  avere dell'acqua/averne ancora? [. . . a-v*ayr*-nay
  an-k*oh*-rah]
  I have to leave tomorrow devo partire
  domani [d*ay*-voh par-t*ee*-ray doh-m*ah*-nee]

hayfever la febbre da fieno [feb-bray dah
fee-ay-noh]
he lui [loo-ee]
  he is è [eh]
  where does he live? dove abita? [doh-vay
  ah-bee-tah]
head la testa
  headache il mal di testa [. . . dee . . .]
  headlight il faro [fah-roh]
  head waiter il capocameriere
  [ka-po-ka-mayr-yeh-ray]
  head wind un vento di prua [. . . dee proo-ah]
health la salute [sa-loo-tay]
  your health! salute!
healthy sano
hear: I can't hear non sento
  hearing aid un apparecchio acustico
  [ap-pa-rayk-yoh a-koos-tee-koh]
heart il cuore [kwo-ray]
  heart attack un colpo al cuore
heat il calore [ka-loh-ray]
  heat stroke un colpo di calore [. . . dee . . .]
heater (electric) la stufetta elettrica
heating il riscaldamento
heavy pesante [pay-san-tay]
heel il calcagno [kal-kan-yoh
  (on shoe) il tacco
  could you put new heels on these? può
  mettere i tacchi a questi? [pwoh met-tay-ray ee
  tak-kee . . .]
hello ciao [chow]
help (noun) aiuto [a-yoo-toh]
  can you help me? mi può aiutare? [mee pwoh
  a-yoo-tah-ray]
  help! aiuto!
her lei [lay]
  have you seen her? l'ha vista? [lah . . .]
  will you give it to her? vuole darglielo?
  [vwoh-lay dar-lee-ay-loh]
  it's her bag/plate è la sua borsa/il suo piatto

....

here qui [kwee]

her(s) il suo (soo-oh], la sua; *(plural)* i suoi [ee swoy-ee], le sue [−ay]
   it's hers è sua/suo

high alto

highway l'autostrada [ow-toh-strah-dah]

hill la collina [koh-lee-nah]
   up/down the hill in salita/discesa [een sa-lee-tah/dee-shay-sah]

him lui [loo-ee]
   I know him lo conosco
   will you give it to him? vuole darglielo? [vwoh-lay dar-lee-ay-loh]

his il suo [soo-oh], la sua; *(plural)* i suoi [ee swoy-ee], le sue [−ay]
   it's his è il suo/la sua [eh . . .]

hit: he hit me mi ha colpito [mee ah kol-pee-toh]

hitchhike *(verb)* fare la'utostop [fah-ray low-toh-stop]
   hitchhiker un autostoppista [ow-toh-stop-pees-tah]

hold tenere [tay-nay-ray]

hole un buco [boo-koh]

home la casa [kah-sah]
   I want to go home voglio andare a casa [vol-yoh an-dah-ray . . .]
   at home a casa
   I am homesick ho nostalgia di casa [o nos-tal-jee-ah dee . . .]

honest onesto
   honestly? davvero?

honey il miele [mee-ay-lay]

honeymoon la luna di miele [. . . dee . . .]

hood *(car)* il cofano [ko-fa-noh]

hope *(noun)* la speranza [spay-ran-tzah]
   I hope that . . . spero che . . . [spay-roh kay]
   I hope so/not spero di sì/di no [. . . dee see/dee . . .]

horizon l'orizzonte [o-reet-tzon-tay]

horn *(car)* il clacson

horrible orribile [or-*ree*-bee-lay]
hors d'oeuvre l'antipasto
horse il cavallo
hospital l'ospedale [os-pay-d*ah*-lay]
host(ess) l'ospite [os-pee-tay]
hot caldo
   (spiced) piccante [peek-k*a*n-tay]
   it's too hot! scotta!
hotel l'albergo
» *TRAVEL TIP: hotels are divided into five*
   categories: deluxe, first, second, third, and
   fourth; hotel lists are issued by the provincial
   Tourist Board and by the local tourist offices
   (aziende autonome di soggiorno)
hotplate il fornello
hot-water bottle la borsa dell'acqua calda
hour l'ora
house la casa [k*ah*-sah]
   housewife la casalinga
how come [k*oh*-may]
   how many? quanti? [kw*a*n-tee]
   how much? quanto? [kw*a*n-toh]
   how often do the buses run? con che
   frequenza partono gli autobus? [kon kay
   fray-kwen-tzah p*a*r-toh-noh lee *ow*-toh-boos]
   how long does it take? quanto ci impiega?
   [. . . chee eem-pee-*ay*-gah]
   how long have you been here? da quanto
   tempo è qua? [. . . eh . . .]
   how are you? come sta? [k*oh*-may stah]
hull lo scafo
humid umido [*oo*-mee-doh]
humor l'umorismo [oo-mo-r*ee*s-moh]
   haven't you got a sense of humor? non ha
   [ah] il senso dell'umorismo?
hundred cento [ch*e*n-toh]
hungry: I'm hungry/not hungry ho fame/non
   ho fame [o f*ah*-may . . .]
hurry: I'm in a hurry ho fretta [o fr*ay*t-tah]
   please hurry! per favore faccia presto!
   [. . . fa-v*oh*-ray f*ah*-chah pres-toh]

hurt: it hurts fa male [fah m*ah*-lay]
   my leg hurts mi fa mal la gamba [mee . . .]
   YOU MAY THEN HEAR . . .
   è un dolore acuto? [eh oon doh-l*oh*-ray
   a-k*oo*-toh] *is it a sharp pain?*
husband: my husband mio marito [m*ee*-oh
   ma-*ree*-toh]
I io [*ee*-oh]
   I am sono
   I leave tomorrow parto domani
ice il ghiaccio [ghee-*ah*-choh]
   ice-cream il gelato [jay-l*ah*-toh]
   iced coffee un caffè freddo [kaf-*feh* . . .]
   with lots of ice con molto ghiaccio
identity papers documenti di identità [. . . dee
   ee-den-tee-t*ah*]
idiot idiota [ee-dee-*oh*-tah]
if se [say]
ignition l'accensione [a-chayn-see-*oh*-nay]
ill malato
   I feel ill mi sento male [mee s*en*-toh m*ah*-lay]
illegal illegale [eel-lay-g*ah*-lay]
illegible illeggibile [eel-lay-jee-bee-lay]
illness una malattia [ma-lat-t*ee*-ah]
immediately immediatamente [–tay]
import importazione [–*oh*-nay]
important importante [–tay]
   it's very important è molto importante
import duty dazio di importazione [d*ah*-tzee-oh
   dee eem-por-ta-tzee-*oh*-nay]
impossible impossibile [eem-pos-s*ee*-bee-lay]
impressive imponente [–n*ay*n-tay]
improve migliorare [meel-yo-r*ah*-ray]
   I want to improve my . . . voglio migliorare il
   mio . . . [*vol*-yoh . . . m*ee*-oh]
in in [een]
   he'll be here in a while sarà qua fra un po'
   in New York a Nuova York
   in 1992 nel 1992 [nel m*ee*l-lay-no-vay-
   chen-toh-no-van-tah-d*oo*-ay]
inch un pollice [pol-lee-chay]

» *TRAVEL TIP: 1 inch = 2.54 cm*

include includere [een-kloo-day-ray]
   does that include breakfast? è compresa la
   prima colazione? [eh kom-pray-sah lah
   pree-mah ko-la-tzee-oh-nay]

incompetent incompetente [–tay]

inconsiderate sconsiderato

incontinent incontinente [–tay]

incredible incredibile [–dee-bee-lay]

incrocio crossroads

indecent indecente [een-day-chen-tay]

independent indipendente [–tay]

India l'India [een-dee-ah]

Indian indiano

indicator la freccia [fray-chah]

indigestion l'indigestione [–oh-nay]

indoors al coperto

industry industria [een-doos-tree-ah]

infection l'infezione [een-fay-tzee-oh-nay]

infectious contagioso [kon-ta-joh-soh]

inflation l'inflazione [een-fla-tzee-oh-nay]

informal senza formalità [sen-tzah
   for-ma-lee-tah]

**information: do you have any information in
   English about...?** ha delle informazioni in
   inglese su...? [ah del-lay een-for-ma-tzee-
   oh-nee een een-glay-say soo]
   is there an information office? c'è un ufficio
   di informazioni? [chay oon oof-fee-choh dee...]

ingresso entrance
   *ingresso gratuito, ingresso libero admission
   free*

inhabitant un abitante [–tay]

injection l'iniezione [een-yay-tzee-oh-nay]

injured ferito [fay-ree-toh]
   he's been injured è stato ferito [eh
   stah-toh...]

injury una lesione [lay-see-oh-nay]

innocent innocente [een-no-chen-tay]

insect un insetto

inside dentro

insist: I insist (on it) insisto [een-*sees*-toh]

insomnia l'insonnia

instant coffee il caffè istantaneo [kaf-*feh* ees-tan-*tah*-nay-oh]

instead invece [een-*vay*-chay]

    instead of... invece di [... dee]

insulating tape il nastro isolante [... ee-so-*lan*-tay]

insulation l'isolamento [ee-so-la-*men*-toh]

insult un insulto [een-*sool*-toh]

insurance l'assicurazione [as-see-koo-ra-tzee-*oh*-nay]

intelligent intelligente [−*tay*]

interesting interessante [−*tay*]

international internazionale [een-tayr-na-tzee-oh-*nah*-lay]

interpret interpretare [−*tah*-ray]

    would you interpret for us? può farci da interprete? [pwoh *far*-chee dah een-*ter*-pray-tay]

into in [een]

introduce: can I introduce...? posso presentare...? [... pray-sayn-*tah*-ray]

invalid *(noun)* un invalido [een-*vah*-lee-doh]

invitation l'invito [een-*vee*-toh]

    thank you for the invitation grazie dell'invito [*grah*-tzee-ay ...]

» TRAVEL TIP: *when invited to an Italian house for a meal it is customary to bring a cake or some ice cream, rather than wine*

invite: can I invite you out? vuoi uscire con me? [vwoy oo-sh*ee*-ray kon may]

invoice la fattura

Ireland l'Irlanda

Irish irlandese [eer-lan-*day*-say]

iron *(clothes)* un ferro da stiro [... st*ee*-roh]

    will you iron these for me? mi può stirare questi? [mee pwoh stee-*rah*-ray kwes-tee]

is è [eh]

island l'isola [*ee*-so-lah]

it esso

it's not working non funziona [non foon-tzee-*oh*-nah]

is it...? è...? [eh]

I'll take it lo prendo

Italian italiano

  an Italian woman un'italiana

  the Italians gli Italiani [lee...]

  I don't speak Italian non parlo l'italiano

Italy l'Italia [ee-t*a*l-yah]

itch il prurito [proo-r*ee*-toh]

  it itches mi fa prurito [mee...]

itemize: would you itemize it for me? me lo dettaglia? [may lo dayt-t*a*l-yah]

IVA sales tax

jack il cricco [kr*ee*k-koh]

jacket una giacca [j*a*k-kah]

jam la marmellata

  traffic jam un ingorgo

January gennaio [jen-n*a*h-yoh]

jaw la mascella [ma-sh*e*l-lah]

jealous geloso [jay-l*oh*-soh]

jeans i jeans

jellyfish una medusa

jetty il molo

jewelry i gioielli [jo-y*e*l-lee]

job un lavoro

joke *(noun)* uno scherzo [sk*a*yr-tzoh]

  you must be joking sta scherzando

journey un viaggio [vee-*a*h-joh]

July luglio [l*oo*l-yoh]

junction un raccordo

June giugno [j*oo*n-yoh]

junk la robaccia [ro-b*a*h-chah]

just: just two solo due [d*oo*-ay]

  just a little solo un po'

  it's just there è lì [lee]

  not just now per ora no

  he was here just now era qua proprio ora

  that's just right è proprio giusto [eh pro-pree-oh j*oo*s-toh]

keep: can I keep it? lo posso tenere?
[. . . tay-n*a*y-ray]
   keep the change tenga il resto
   you didn't keep your promise non ha
   mantenuto la promessa [. . . ah . . .]
   it keeps on breaking si continua a rompere
   [see kon-*tee*-noo-ah ah rom-pay-ray]
ketchup il ketchup
kettle il bollitore [bol-lee-*toh*-ray]
key la chiave [kee-*ah*-vay]
kidney il rene [r*a*y-nay]
   (meat) il rognone [ron-*yoh*-nay]
kill uccidere [oo-ch*ee*-day-ray]
kilo un chilo [k*ee*-loh]

» *TRAVEL TIP: conversion:* $\frac{kilos}{5} \times 11 = pounds$

kilos	1	1½	5	6	7	8	9
pounds	2.2	3.3	11	13.2	15.4	17.6	19.8

kilometer un chilometro [kee-l*oh*-may-troh]

» *TRAVEL TIP: conversion:* $\frac{kilometers}{8} \times 5 = miles$

kilometers	1	5	10	20	50	100
miles	0.62	3.11	6.2	12.4	31	62

kind: that's very kind of you è molto gentile
   da parte sua [eh . . . jen-*tee*-lay dah p*a*r-tay . . .]
   what kind of . . . ? che tipo di . . . ? [kay-*tee*-poh
   dee]
kiss un bacio [b*a*h-choh]
kitchen la cucina [koo-ch*ee*-nay]
knee il ginocchio [jee-n*o*k-yoh]
knife il coltello [kol-t*e*l-loh]
knock bussare [boos-s*a*h-ray]
   there's a knocking noise from the engine il
   motore dà dei colpi [eel mo-t*oh*-ray dah day
   kol-pee]
know sapere [sa-p*a*y-ray]
   (be acquainted with) conoscere [ko-n*o*h-
   shay-ray]
   I don't know non so

I don't know the area non conosco queste parti [. . . kwes-tay par-tee]

label l'etichetta [ay-tee-kayt-tah]

laces *(shoes)* i lacci [lah-chee]

lacquer la lacca

ladies *(toilet)* donne

» *TRAVEL TIP: only written: ask for* la toilette [twalet]

lady una signora [seen-yo-rah]

lake il lago [lah-goh]

lamb l'agnello [an-yel-loh]

lamp la lampada [lam-pa-dah]

   lampshade il paralume [−loo-may]

   lamppost il lampione [lam-pee-oh-nay]

land *(noun)* la terra

lane *(car)* la corsia [kor-see-ah]

language la lingua [leen-gwah]

large grande [gran-day]

laryngitis la laringite [la-reen-jee-tay]

last ultimo [ool-tee-moh]

   last year/week l'anno scorso/la settimana scorsa

   last night la notte scorsa [−tay]

   at last! finalmente! [fee-nal-men-tay]

late: sorry I'm late scusi per il ritardo [skoo-zee . . .]

   it's a bit late è un po' tardi [eh . . . tar-dee]

   please hurry, I'm late in fretta per favore, sono in ritardo [. . . payr fa-voh-ray]

   at the latest al più tardi [al pew . . .]

   later più tardi

   see you later a più tardi

latitude la latitudine [−too-dee-nay]

laugh *(verb)* ridere [ree-day-ray]

laundrette una lavanderia automatica [la-van-day-ree-ah ow-toh-mah-tee-kah]

» *TRAVEL TIP: if you can't find a laundrette look for a "lavasecco" (dry cleaner's)*

   laundry detergent il detersivo [day-tayr-see-voh]

lavori in corso men at work

law la legge [leh-jay]

lawyer l'avvocato

laxative un lassativo

lazy pigro [pee-groh]

leaf la foglia [fol-yah]

leak: there's a leak in my ceiling il mio soffitto fa acqua [mee-oh sof-feet-toh . . .]

   it leaks ha una perdita [ah oo-nah per-dee-tah]

learn: I want to learn . . . voglio imparare . . . [vol-yoh eem-pa-rah-ray]

lease *(verb)* affittare [−tah-ray]

least: not in the least proprio per niente [. . . nee-en-tay]

   at least almeno [al-may-noh]

leather la pelle [pel-lay]

   leather soles suole di cuoio [swo-lay dee kwo-yoh]

leave: we're leaving tomorrow partiamo domani

   when does the bus leave? quando parte l'autobus? [. . . par-tay low-toh-boos]

   I left two shirts in my room ho lasciato due camice in camera mia [o la-shah-toh doo-ay ka-mee-chay een kah-may-rah mee-ah]

   can I leave this here? posso lasciarlo qua?

left sinistra [see-nees-trah]

   on the left a sinistra

   left-handed mancino [man-chee-noh]

left luggage (office) il deposito bagagli [day-po-see-toh ba-gal-yee]

leg la gamba

legal legale [lay-gah-lay]

lemon un limone [lee-moh-nay]

lemonade una limonata [lee-mo-nah-tah]

lend: will you lend me your . . . ? mi presta il suo . . . ? [mee . . .]

lengthen allungare [al-loon-gah-ray]

lens la lente [len-tay]

Lent la Quaresima [kwa-ray-see-mah]
less meno [may-noh]
  less than meno di [...dee]
  less than you think meno che non pensi
  [...kay...]
let: let me help aspetti che l'aiuto [...kay
  la-yoo-toh]
  let me go! mi lasci andare! [mee lah-shee
  an-dah-ray]
  will you let me off here? mi fa scendere qua?
  [mee fah shen-day-ray...]
  let's go andiamo
  let me have a look mi faccia vedere [mee
  fah-chah vay-day-ray]
letter la lettera [let-tay-rah]
  are there any letters for me? ci sono lettere
  per me? [chee...may]
lettuce l'insalata
liable *(responsible)* responsabile
  [res-pon-sah-bee-lay]
libero vacant
library la biblioteca [bee-blee-o-tay-kah]
licence il permesso
  license plate la targa
lid il coperchio [ko-per-kee-oh]
lie *(noun)* la menzogna [mayn-tzoh-yah]
  can he lie down for a bit? può andare a
  riposarsi per u po'? [pwoh an-dah-ray...]
life la vita [vee-tah]
  life insurance l'assicurazione sulla vita
  [as-see-koo-ra-tzee-oh-nay sool-lah...]
  life jacket la cintura di salvataggio
  [cheen-too-rah dee sal-va-tah-joh]
  lifeboat la scialuppa di salvataggio
  [sha-loop-pah dee...]
  lifeguard il bagnino [ban-yee-noh]
lift: do you want a lift? vuole un passaggio?
  [vwoh-lay oon pas-sah-joh]
  could you give me a lift? mi può dare un
  passaggio? [mee pwoh dah-ray...]

....

light *(not heavy)* leggero [lay-jay-roh]
   the lights aren't working la luce non
   funziona [la loo-chay non foon-tzee-oh-nah]
   (car) i fari non funzionano [ee fah-ree non
   foon-tzee-oh-na-noh]
   have you got a light? ha da accendere?
   [ah da a-chen-day-ray]
   when it gets light quando fa giorno
   [...jor-noh]
   light bulb la lampadina [−dee-nah]
   the light bulb's gone out la lampadina è
   rotta [lam-pa-dee-nah eh...]
   light meter l'esposimetro [les-po-see-
   may-troh]
like: would you like...? vuole...? [vwoh-lay]
   I'd like a coffee vorrei un caffè [vor-ray oon
   kaf-feh]
   I'd like to go vorrei partire [...−tee-ray]
   I like you mi sei simpatico [mee say seem-
   pah-tee-koh]
   I like it/I don't like it mi piace/non mi piace
   [...mee pee-ah-chay]
   what's it like? com'è? [koh-meh]
   one like this uno come questo
   [...koh-may...]
   do it like this lo faccia così [lo fah-chah
   ko-see]
lime il cedro [chay-droh]
line la linea [lee-nay-ah]
   (for tickets, etc.) la coda
lips le labbra
   lipstick il rossetto
   lip salve il burro di cacao [boor-roh dee
   ka-kah-oh]
liqueur un liquore [lee-kwoh-ray]
» TRAVEL TIP: **Sambuca:** *sort of anisette;* **amaro:**
   bitter, made with herbs; **Fernet:** *rather*
   medicinal flavor, great for upset stomach or
   hangover; **Strega:** *unique flavor, herb-based*
list *(noun)* la lista
listen ascoltare [−tah-ray]

liter un litro
» *TRAVEL TIP:* 1 *liter* = 1.06 *quarts* = 0.22 *gals*
little *(adjective)* piccolo
   a little ice/a little more un po' di ghiaccio/un
   po' di più [. . . dee ghee-*ah*-choh/ . . . dee pew]
   just a little solo un po'
live vivere [vee-vay-ray]
   I live in Boston/in America abito a
   Boston/in America [*ah*-bee-toh . . .]
   where do you live? dove abita? [d*oh*-vay
   ah-bee-tah]
liver il fegato [f*ay*-ga-toh]
lizard la lucertola [loo-ch*ayr*-toh-lah]
loaf una pagnotta [pan-y*ot*-tah]
lobster l'aragosta
local: could we try a local wine? possiamo
   provare un vino locale? [. . . pro-v*ah*-ray oon
   vee-noh lo-k*ah*-lay]
   a local restaurant un ristorante locale
   is it made locally? è fatto sul posto? [eh . . .]
lock la serratura
   the lock's broken la serratura è rotta
   I've locked myself out mi sono chiuso fuori
   [mee s*oh*-noh kee-*oo*-soh fw*oh*-ree]
London Londra
lonely: are you lonely? ti senti solo? [tee . . .]
long lungo [loon-goh]
   we'd like to stay longer vorremmo stare più
   a lungo [. . . st*ah*-ray pew . . .]
   that was long ago questo era tanto tempo fa
   [. . . *eh*-rah]
longitude la longitudine [lon-jee-t*oo*-dee-nay]
look: you look tired mi sembra stanco
   [mee . . .]
   I'm looking forward to . . . non vedo l'ora
   di . . . [. . . v*ay*-doh . . . dee]
   I'm just looking sto guardando
   [. . . gwar-d*an*-doh]
   I'm looking for . . . cerco . . . [ch*ayr*-koh]
   look at that guarda quello [gw*ar*-dah . . .]
   look out! attento!

....

loose allentato
   (clothes) largo
lose perdere [p*a*yr-day-ray]
   I've lost my... ho perso il mio... [o p*a*yr-soh
   eel m*ee*-oh]
   excuse me, I'm lost scusi, mi sono perso
   [sk*oo*-zee, mee...]
lost property (office) oggetti smarriti [o-jet-tee
   smar-r*ee*-tee]
lot: a lot/not a lot molto/non molto
   a lot of potato chips/wine tante
   patatine/tanto vino [t*a*n-tay pa-ta-t*ee*-nay/
   t*a*n-toh v*ee*-noh]
   lots (of) un sacco (di) [...dee]
   a lot more expensive molto più caro
   [...pew...]
lotion la lozione [lo-tzee-*oh*-nay]
loud: could you speak louder? può parlare più
   forte? [pwoh par-l*ah*-ray pew for-tay]
love: I love you ti amo [tee *ah*-moh]
   do you love me? mi ami? [mee *ah*-mee]
   he's in love è innamorato [eh...]
   I love this wine questo vino me piace
   moltissimo [kwes-toh v*ee*-noh mee
   pee-*ah*-chay...]
lovely bello
low basso
low beams gli anabbaglianti [lee
   a-nab-bal-y*a*n-tee]
luck fortuna [for-t*oo*-nah]
   good luck! buona fortuna! [bw*o*-nah...]
lucky fortunato [for-too-n*ah*-toh]
   you're lucky sei fortunato [say...]
   that's lucky che fortuna [kay...]
luggage il bagaglio [ba-g*a*l-yoh]
lumbago la lombaggine [lom-b*ah*-jee-nay]
lump *(in the body)* on gonfiore
   [gon-fee-*oh*-ray]
lunch il pranzo [pr*a*n-tzoh]
   (in Rome) la colazione [−tzee-*oh*-nay]
lung il polmone [pol-m*oh*-nay]

luxurious lussuoso
luxury il lusso [loos-soh]
  a luxury hotel un albergo de [dee] lusso
mad matto
madam signora [seen-yoh-rah]
made-to-measure fatto su misura [. . . soo
  mee-soo-rah]
magazine una rivista [ree-vees-tah]
magnificent magnifico [man-yee-fee-koh]
maid la cameriera [ka-may-ree-eh-rah]
maiden name il nome da signorina [noh-may
  dah seen-yo-ree-nah]
mail la posta; **is there any mail for me?** c'è
  posta per me? [cheh . . . may]
mailbox la cassetta delle lettere
mainland il continente [−nen-tay]
main road la strada principale
  [. . . preen-chee-pah-lay]
make fare [fah-ray]
  will we make it in time? ce la faremo in
  tempo? [chay la fa-ray-moh . . .]
makeup il trucco [trook-koh]
man un uomo [wo-moh]
manager il direttore [dee-ray-toh-ray]
  can I see the manager? posso parlare col
  direttore? [. . . par-lah-ray . . .]
manicure una manicure [ma-nee-koo-ray]
manners le maniere [man-yay-ray]
  haven't you got any manners? non ha un po'
  di educazione? [non ah oon po dee
  ay-doo-ka-tzee-oh-nay]
many molti [mol-tee]
map: a map of Italy una carta d'Italia
  a map of Rome una pianta di Roma
  [pee-an-tah dee . . .]
March marzo [mar-tzoh]
margarine la margarina [mar-ga-ree-nah]
marina il porto turistico [. . . too-rees-tee-koh]
mark: there's a mark on it c'è un segno [cheh
  oon sayn-yoh]
marketplace il mercato [mayr-kah-toh]

marmalade la marmellata d'arance
[mar-mel-*lah*-tah da-*ran*-chay]
married sposato
marry: will you marry me? mi vuoi sposare?
[mee vw*oy*-ee spo-*sah*-ray]
marvelous meraviglioso [may-ra-veel-*yoh*-soh]
mascara il mascara
mashed potatoes il purè de patate [poo-*reh* dee
pa-*tah*-tay]
massage il massaggio [mas-*sah*-joh]
mast l'albero [al-bay-roh]
mat *(door)* lo stuoino [stwo-*ee*-noh]
(table) un sottopiatto
match un fiammifero [fee-am-m*ee*-fay-roh]
(short waxed match used by smokers) un cerino
[chay-*ree*-noh]
a box of matches una scatola di fiammiferi
[sk*ah*-toh-lah dee . . .]
material la stoffa
matter: it doesn't matter non importa
what's the matter? cosa c'è? [. . . cheh]
mattress il materasso
mature maturo [ma-*too*-roh]
maximum massimo [m*as*-see-moh]
May maggio [m*ah*-joh]
may: may I have . . . ? potrei avere . . . ? [po-tr*ay*
a v*ay*-ray]
maybe forse [for-say]
mayonnaise la maionese [mah-yo-n*ay*-say]
me: with me con me [kon may]
he knows me mi conosce [mee ko-n*oh*-shay]
it's me sono io [. . . *ee*-oh]
meal il pasto
mean: what does this mean? cosa vuol dire?
[. . . vwol d*ee*-ray]
by all means! certamente! [chayr-ta-m*en*-tay]
measles il morbillo
German measles la rosolia [ro-so-l*ee*-ah]
measurements le misure [mee-*soo*-ray]
meat la carne [k*ar*-nay]

mechanic: is there a mechanic here? c'è un
meccanico qui? [cheh oon mayk-*kah*-nee-koh
kwee]
medicine la medicina [may-dee-chee-na]
Mediterranean il Mediterraneo [−*rah*-nay-oh]
meet: when shall we meet? a che ora ci
ritroviamo? [ah kay *oh*-rah chee . . .]
I met him in the street l'ho incontrato per
strada [lo . . .]; **pleased to meet you** piacere
[pee-ah-ch*ay*-ray]
meeting un incontro
melon un melone [may-l*oh*-nay]
member un socio [*so*-choh]
how do I become a member? come si
diventa soci? [k*oh*-may see dee-ven-tah s*o*-chee]
men gli uomini [lee wo-mee-nee]
mend: can you mend this? può aggiustare
questo? [pwoh a-joos-t*ah*-ray . . .]
mention: don't mention it prego [pr*ay*-goh]
menu il menù [may-n*oo*]
can I have the menu, please? posso avere il
menù, per favore? [. . . a-v*ay*-ray . . . payr
fa-v*oh*-ray]
» *TRAVEL TIP: see pages 74–75*
mess: what a mess! che pasticcio! [kay
pas-t*ee*-choh]
my room is a mess la mia camera è in
disordine [lah m*ee*-ah k*ah*-may-rah eh een
dee-s*or*-dee-nay]
message: are there any messages for me? ci
sono messaggi per me? [chee s*oh*-noh
mays-s*ah*-jee payr may]
can I leave a message for . . . ? posso lasciare
un messaggio per . . . ? [. . . la-sh*ah*-ray . . .]
meter un metro [m*ay*-troh]
» *TRAVEL TIP: 1 meter = 39.37 in. = 1.09 yd.*
metropolitana subway
midday mezzogiorno [met-tzo-jor-noh]
middle mezzo [m*et*-tzoh]
in the middle nel mezzo

....

midnight mezzanotte [met-tza-not-tay]

might: I might be late può darsi che faccia tardi [pwoh dar-see kay fah-chah tar-dee]

he might have gone può darsi che se ne sia andato [. . . kay say nay see-ah an-dah-toh]

migraine l'emicrania [ay-mee-kran-yah]

mild *(weather)* mite [mee-tay]

(cheese) dolce [dol-chay]

mile un miglio [meel-yoh]

» *TRAVEL TIP: conversion:* $\dfrac{miles}{5} \times 8 = kilometers$

miles	½	1	3	5	10	50	100
kilometers	0.8	1.6	4.8	8	16	80	160

milk il latte [lat-tay]

a glass of milk un bicchiere di latte [oon beek-yeh-ray dee . . .]

milkshake un frappé [frap-pay]

millimeter un millimetro [meel-lee-may-troh]

million un milione [meel-yo-nay]

minced meat la carne tritata [kar-nay tree-tah-tah]

mind: I've changed my mind ho cambiato idea [o kam-bee-ah-toh ee-day-ah]

I don't mind non importa

I don't mind driving sono disposto a guidare [. . . gwee-dah-ray]

do you mind if I . . . ? le spiace se . . . ? [lay spee-ah-chay say]

never mind non fa niente [. . . nee-en-tay]

mine mio [mee-oh]

that's mine questo è mio

mineral water l'acqua minerale [–rah-lay]

minimum minimo [mee-nee-moh]

minus meno [may-noh]

it's minus 3 degrees ci sono tre gradi sotto zero [chee soh-noh tray grah-dee sot-toh tzay-roh]

minute minuto [mee-noo-toh]

in a minute subito [soo-bee-toh]

just a minute un momento
mirror lo specchia [spek-yoh]
Miss signorina [seen-yoh-ree-nah]
miss: I miss you mi manchi [mee-man-kee]
   Carlo's missing manca Carlo
   there's a...missing manca un...
mist la foschia [fos-kee-ah]
mistake uno sbaglio [sbal-yoh]
   I think you've made a mistake credo che si
   sia sbagliato [kray-doh kay see see-ah
   sbal-yah-toh]
misunderstanding un malinteso [−tay-soh]
modern moderno [−ayr-noh]
mom mamma
Monday lunedì [loo-nay-dee]
money il denaro
   I've lost my money ho perso i soldi
   [o payr-soh ee sol-dee]
   I have no money non ho denaro [...o...]
   they've taken all my money mi hanno
   rubato tutto il denaro [mee an-noh...]
month un mese [may-say]
moon la luna [loo-nay]
moorings gli ormeggi [lee or-may-jee]
moped il motorino [−ree-noh]
more più [pew]
   can I have some more? posso averne ancora?
   [...a-vayr-nay...]
   more wine, please ancora del vino per favore
   [...vee-noh payr fa-voh-ray]
   no more basta [bas-tah]
   more comfortable più comodo
   more than più di [...dee]
morning il mattino [−tee-noh]
   good morning buon giorno [bwon jor-noh]
   this morning questa mattina
   in the morning di mattina [dee...]
   tomorrow morning domattina
mosquito una zanzara

Antipasti: Starters
affettati misti *assorted cold meats*
prosciutto e melone *ham and melon*
insalata di frutti di mare *seafood salad*

Primi piatti: Soups and pasta
stracciatella *clear soup with eggs and cheese*
minestrone *thick vegetable soup*
zuppa de pesce *fish soup*
spaghetti alla carbonara *with egg and bacon
    sauce*
spaghetti al sugo *with meat sauce*
spaghetti al pomodoro *with tomato sauce*
lasagne al forno *layers of pasta and meat sauce
    covered with cheese and baked*
cannelloni *pasta stuffed with meat sauce and
    baked*
ravioli *pasta squares stuffed with meat or other
    savory filling, served with a sauce*
gnocchi *potato dumplings*
risotto alla milanese *rice cooked in white wine
    and saffron with mushrooms and cheese*

Carni: Meat dishes
bistecca ai ferri/alla pizzaiola/alla
    fiorentina *grilled steak/steak with tomato
    sauce/grilled T-bone steak*
cotoletta alla milanese *veal cutlet in egg and
    breadcrumbs*
cotoletta d'agnello/di vitello *lamb/veal cutlet*
ossobuco *knuckle of veal in wine and tomato
    sauce*
saltimbocca alla romana *veal escalopes with ham
    and sage*
spezzatino di vitello *veal stew*

Pollame: Poultry
anitra all'arancio *duck in orange sauce*
pollo arrosto *roast chicken*
pollo alla cacciatora *chicken in a wine, onion,
    and tomato sauce*

Pesce: Fish
baccalà *salt cod*
calamari in umido *squid in wine, garlic, and
tomato sauce*
fritto misto *mixed fried fish*
polipo ai ferri *grilled octopus*
sogliola al burro *sole in butter sauce*
trota ai ferri *grilled trout*

Contorni: Vegetables
patate: arrosto/fritte/cotte *potatoes:
roast/fried/boiled*
purè di patate *mashed potatoes*
insalata mista *mixed salad*
pomodori al gratin *grilled tomatoes*
fagiolini al burro *green beans in butter*
finocchi al forno *fennel with cheese, browned in
the oven*
melanzane al forno *baked eggplant in cheese
sauce*
zucchini fritti *fried zucchini*

Formaggi: Cheese
Bel Paese *soft, full fat cheese*
caciotta *hard, medium fat cheese*
gorgonzola *soft, tangy blue cheese*
mozzarella *soft, sweet cheese made from buffalo's
milk*
parmigiano *Parmesan*

Frutta e dolci: Desserts
macedonia *fruit salad*
cassata *ice cream with candied fruit*
gelato *ice cream*
torta di mele/ciliege etc. *apple/cherry etc. tart*
zabaione *frothy dessert made with egg yolks,
sugar, and marsala wine*

most: I like it the most mi piace più di tutto
[mee pee-*ah*-chay pew dee *toot*-toh]
 I like you the most mi piaci più di tutti
[. . . pee-*ah*-chee . . .]
 most of the time la maggior parte del tempo
[ma-jor par-tay . . .]
 most of the people il più della gente [d*e*l-lah
j*e*n-tay]
motel un motel
mother: my mother mia madre [m*ee*-ah
m*ah*-dray]
motor il motore [−ray]
motorbike la motocicletta [−chee-kl*a*yt-tah]
motorboat il motoscafo
motorcyclist il motociclista [−chee-kl*ee*s-tah]
motorist un automobilista [ow-toh-mo-bee-
l*ee*s-tah]
mountain la montagna [mon-t*a*n-yah]
mountaineer un alpinista
mountaineering l'alpinismo
mouse un topo
moustache i baffi [ee . . .]
mouth la bocca
move: don't move non si muova [non see
mw*o*-vah]
 could you move your car? può spostare la
macchina? [pwoh spos-t*ah*-ray lah
m*a*k-kee-nah]
movie un film
 let's go to the movies andiamo al cinema
[an-dee-*ah*-moh al ch*ee*-nay-mah]
movie theater il cinema [ch*ee*-nay-mah]
Mr. signor, Sig. [seen-y*o*r]
Mrs. signora, Sig.ra [seen-y*o*-rah]
Ms *no equivalent*
much molto
 much better/much more molto meglio/molto
di più [. . . m*e*l-yoh . . . dee pew]
 not much non molto
muffler *(car)* il silenziatore [see-len-tzee-a-t*oh*-ray]

mug: I've been mugged sono stato assalito e
derubato [. . . st*ah*-toh as-sa-l*ee*-toh ay
day-roo-b*ah*-toh]
muscle il muscolo [m*oo*s-ko-loh]
museum il museo [m*oo*-s*eh*-oh]
mushrooms i funghi [f*oo*n-ghee]
music la musica [m*oo*-see-kah]
must: I must have . . . devo avere . . . [d*ay*-voh
a-v*ay*-ray]
   I must not eat . . . non devo mangiare . . .
   [man-j*ah*-ray]
   you must do it deve farlo [d*ay*-vay . . .]
   must I . . . ? devo . . . ?
mustard la senape [s*ay*-na-pay]
my il mio [m*ee*-oh]; la mia; *(plural)* i miei [ee
mee-*eh*-ee]; le mie [−ay]
nail *(finger)* l'unghia [*oo*n-ghee-ah]
   (wood) il chiodo [kee-*o*-doh]
   nail clippers un tagliaunghie
   [tal-yah-*oo*n-ghee-ay]
   nail file la limetta da unghie
   [lee-m*ay*t-tah . . .]
   nail polish lo smalto per unghie
   nail scissors le forbicine da unghie
   [for-bee-ch*ee*-nay]
naked nudo [n*oo*-doh]
name il nome [n*oh*-may]
   first name il nome di battesimo [n*oh*-may
   dee bat-t*ay*-see-moh]
   my name is . . . mi chiamo . . . [mee
   kee-*ah*-moh]
   what's you name? come si chiama? [k*oh*-may
   see kee-*ah*-mah]
napkin il tovagliolo [toh-val-y*o*-loh]
narrow stretto
national nazionale [na-tzee-oh-n*ah*-lay]
   nationality la nazionalità [−tah]
natural naturale [na-too-r*ah*-lay]
naughty: don't be naughty non essere
impertinente [non *e*s-say-ray . . . −tay]

....

near: is it near? è vicino? [eh vee-ch*ee*-noh]
  near here qui vicino [kwee...]
  do you go near...? va dalle parti di...?
[vah d*a*l-lay p*a*r-tee dee]
  where's the nearest...? dov'è il più
vicino...? [doh-v*e*h il pew...]
nearly quasi [kw*a*h-see]
neat *(drink)* liscio [l*ee*-shoh]
necessary necessario [nay-chays-s*a*h-ree-oh]
  it's not necessary non è necessario
neck il collo
  necklace la collana
need: I need a... ho bisogno di...
[o bee-s*o*nn-yoh dee]
needle un ago [*a*h-goh]
negotiations le trattative [lay trat-ta-t*ee*-vay]
neighbor il vicino [vee-ch*ee*-noh]
neither: neither of them nessuno dei due
[...day d*oo*-ay]
  neither...nor... né...né...
[nay...nay...]
  neither do I neanche io [nay-*a*n-kay *ee*-oh]
nephew: my nephew mio nipote [m*ee*-oh
nee-p*oh*-tay]
nervous nervoso
net la rete [r*ay*-tay]
  net price prezzo netto [pr*e*t-tzoh]
never mai [m*a*h-ee]
  I never go there non ci vado mai [...chee
v*a*h-doh...]
new nuovo [nw*o*-voh]
  New Year l'Anno Nuovo
  Happy New Year! Buon Anno! [bwon...]
  New Year's Eve la sera di Capodanno
[...s*ay*-rah dee...]
New Zealand la Nuova Zelanda
[...tzay-l*a*n-dah]
New Zealander un neozelandese
[nay-oh-tzay-lan-d*ay*-say]
news le notizie [no-t*ee*-tzee-ay]

newsstand il giornalaio [jor-na-l*ah*-yoh]
newspaper il giornale [jor-n*ah*-lay]
do you have any English newspapers? ha
dei giornali inglesi? [ah day jor-n*ah*-lee
een-gl*ay*-see]
next: the next day il giorno dopo [jor-noh . . .]
  sit next to me si sieda vicino a me [see
  see-*eh*-dah vee-ch*ee*-noh ah may]
  please stop at the next corner per favore si
  fermi al prossimo angolo [payr fa-v*oh*-ray see
  f*er*-mee al pros-see-moh *a*n-go-loh]
  see you next year arrivederci all'anno
  prossimo [ar-ree-vay-d*ay*r-chee . . .]
nice: a nice person una persona simpatica
  [. . . seem-p*ah*-tee-kah]
  a nice day una bella giornata
  [. . . jor-n*ah*-tah]
niece: my niece mia nipote [m*ee*-ah nee-p*oh*-tay]
night la notte [n*ot*-tay]
  good night buona notte [bw*o*-nah . . .]
  at night di notte [dee . . .]
  is there a good nightclub here? c'è un buon
  nightclub qua? [cheh oon bwon . . .]
  nightgown la camicia da notte
  [ka-m*ee*-chah . . .]
  night porter il portiere di notte
  [por-tee-*ay*-ray dee . . .]
nine nove [n*o*-vay]
  nineteen diciannove [dee-chan-n*o*-vay]
  nineteen ninety two/three
  millenovecentonovantadue/tré
  [m*ee*l-lay-no-vay-ch*e*n-toh-noh-van-tah-d*oo*-ay
  /tr*ay*]
no no
  there's no water non c'è acqua [non cheh . . .]
  no way! certamente no! [chayr-ta-m*e*n-tay . . .]
  I have no money non ho denaro [. . . o . . .]
nobody nessuno
  nobody saw it non l'ha visto nessuno [non
  lah . . .]

....

noisy rumoroso
   our room's too noisy la nostra camera è
   troppo rumorosa [. . . k*ah*-may-rah eh . . .]
non toccare *do not touch*
none nessuno
   none of them nessuno di essi [. . . dee *es*-see]
nonsense sciocchezze [shok-k*ay*t-tzay]
normal normale [nor-m*ah*-lay]
north nord
Northern Ireland l'Irlanda del Nord
nose il naso
   nosebleed il sangue al naso [s*an*-gway . . .]
not non
   I'm not hungry non ho fame [non o f*ah*-may]
   not that one non quello
   not me io no [*ee*-oh . . .]
   I don't smoke non fumo [non f*oo*-moh]
   I didn't order it non l'ho ordinato [non lo . . .]
nothing niente [nee-*en*-tay]
November novembre [–bray]
now adesso
nowhere da nessuna parte [. . . p*ar*-tay]
nudist il nudista [noo-d*ee*s-tah]
   nudist beach la spiaggia per nudisti
   [spee-*ah*-jah . . .]
nuisance: it's a nuisance! è una seccatura!
[eh . . .]
   this man's being a nuisance quest'uomo sta
   dando fastidio [kwest-wo-moh . . . fas-t*ee*-dee-oh]
numb intorpidito [een-tor-pee-d*ee*-toh]
number il numero [n*oo*-may-roh] *see page 127*
nurse l'infermiera [enn-fer-mee-*ay*-rah]
nut la noce [n*oh*-chay]
   (for bolt) il dado [d*ah*-doh]
oar il remo [r*ay*-moh]
obligatory obbligatorio [–t*oh*-ree-oh]
obviously ovviamente [–*men*-tay]
occasionally a volte [vol-tay]
occupato *occupied*
   (telephone, toilet) occupato

....

occupied: is this seat occupied? è occupato?
  [eh . . .]
o'clock *see* **time**
October ottobre [ot-*toh*-bray]
octopus il polipo [po-lee-poh]
odd *(number)* dispari [*dees*-pa-ree]
  (strange) strano
odometer il contachilometri [—kee-lo-may-tree]
of di [dee]
off: it just came off si è staccato [see . . .]
  10% off uno sconto del dieci per cento
  [. . . dee-*ay*-chee payr chen-toh]
offense un'offesa
office l'ufficio [oof-*fee*-choh]
official *(noun)* un ufficiale [oof-fee-ch*ah*-lay]
often spesso
oil l'olio [ol-yoh]
  I'm losing oil perdo l'olio
  will you change the oil? mi cambia l'olio?
  [mee k*am*-bee-ah . . .]
ointment la pomata
OK okay
old vecchio [v*ek*-yoh]
  how old are you? quanti anni hai? [kw*an*-tee
  an-nee *ah*-ee]
olive l'oliva [o-*lee*-vah]
  olive oil l'olio d'oliva [ol-yoh . . .]
omelette la frittata
on su [soo]
  I haven't got it on me non l'ho qui [non lo
  kwee]
  on Friday venerdì [—dee]
  on television alla televisione
  [. . . tay-lay-vee-see-*oh*-nay]
once una volta
  at once subito [s*oo*-bee-t*oh*]
one uno
  the red one quello rosso
one-way: one-way ticket to . . . un'andata
  per . . . [oon an-d*ah*-tah . . .]

....

onion una cipolla [chee-pol-lah]
only solo
   the only one l'unico [loo-nee-koh]
open *(adjective)* aperto
   I can't open it non riesco ad aprirlo [non
   ree-ays-koh . . .]
   when do you open? A che ora aprite? [ah
   kay oh-ray a-pree-tay]
opera l'opera [o-pay-rah]
operation l'operazione [o-pay-ra-tzee-oh-nay]
   will I need an operation? ho bisogno di una
   operazione? [o bee-sonn-yoh dee . . .]
operator *(phone)* il centralino [chen-tra-lee-noh]
» *TRAVEL TIP: for information dial 181*
opposite: opposite the hotel davanti all'albergo
optician l'ottico
or o
orange *(fruit)* l'arancia [a-ran-chah]
   (color) arancione [a-ran-choh-nay]
   orange juice succo d'arancia [sook-koh . . .]
order: could we order now? possiamo ordinare
   adesso? [. . . or-dee-nah-ray . . .]
   thank you, we've already ordered grazie,
   abbiamo già ordinato [grah-tzee-ay
   ab-bee-ah-moh djah . . .]
other: the other one quell'altro
   do you have any others? ne ha degli altri?
   [nay ah day-lee al-tree]
otherwise altrimenti [−tee]
ought: I ought to go dovrei andare [doh-vray
   an-dah-ray]
ounce un'oncia [on-chah]
» *TRAVEL TIP: 1 ounce = 28.35 grams*
our il nostro; la nostra
   that's ours è nostro
out: we're out of gas siamo senza benzina
   [see-ah-moh sen-tzah ben-tzee-nah]
   get out! fuori! [fwoh-ree]
outboard *(motor)* il fuoribordo [fwo-ree-bor-doh]
outdoors all'aperto

outlet *(electrical)* la presa (di corrente) [pr*a*y-sah dee kor-ren-tay]

outside: can we sit outside? possiamo sederci fuori? [. . . say-d*a*yr-chee fw*oh*-ree]

over: over here/there qui/la [kwee/lah]
he's over 40 ha più di quarant'anni [ah pew dee kwa-ran-t*a*n-nee]
it's all over è tutto finito [eh . . .]

overboard: man overboard! uomo in mare! [w*o*-moh een m*ah*-ray]

overcharge: you've overcharged me mi ha fatto pagare troppo [mee ah f*a*t-toh pa-g*ah*-ray . . .]

overcooked troppo cotto

overexposed sovraesposto [so-vra-ays-p*o*s-toh]

overnight *(stay)* per una notte [. . . n*o*t-tay]
we've traveled overnight abbiamo viaggiato di notte [. . . vee-a-j*ah*-toh dee . . .]

oversleep: I overslept non mi sono svegliato [non mee s*oh*-noh svayl-y*ah*-toh]

overtake sorpassare [sor-pas-s*ah*-ray]

owe: what do I owe you? quanto le devo? [. . . lay d*a*y-voh]

own *(adjective)* proprio [pro-pree-oh]
my own . . . il mio proprio . . . [m*ee*-oh . . .]
I'm on my own sono da solo

owner il proprietario [pro-pree-ay-t*ah*-ree-oh]

oxygen l'ossigeno [os-s*ee*-jay-noh]

oysters le ostriche [os-tree-kay]**pack: I haven't packed yet** non ho ancora fatto i bagagli [ee ba-g*a*l-yee]

page *(of book)* la pagina [p*ah*-jee-nah]
could you page him? può farlo cercare? [pwoh far-loh chayr-k*ah*-ray]

pain il dolore [doh-l*oh*-ray]
I've got a pain in my . . . ho [o] un dolore al . . .

painkillers gli analgesici [lee a-nal-j*a*y-see-chee]

painting un dipinto [dee-p*ee*n-toh]

pair un paio [p*ah*-yoh]

....

pajamas il pigiama [pee-j*ah*-mah]
pale pallido [p*a*l-lee-doh]
pancake la frittella
panties le mutandine [moo-tan-d*ee*-nay]
pants i pantaloni [ee . . .]
paper la carta
   (newspaper) il giornale [jor-n*ah*-lay]
parcel il pacco
parcheggio *parking*
pardon *(didn't understand)* come? [koh-may]
   I beg your pardon *(sorry)* scusi [sk*oo*-zee]
parents: my parents i miei genitori
   [ee mee-*eh*-ee jay-nee-t*oh*-ree]
park il parco
   where can I park my car? dove posso
   parcheggiare? [d*oh*-vay pos-soh par-kay-
   j*ah*-ray]
parking lot un parcheggio [par-k*a*y-joh]
part la parte [p*a*r-tay]
partenze *departures*
partner il compagno [kon-p*a*n-yoh]
party *(group)* la comitiva [ko-mee-t*ee*-vah]
   (celebration) la festa
   I'm with the . . . party sono con la comitiva
   di . . . [. . . dee]
pass *(mountain)* il passo
   he's passed out è svenuto [eh . . .]
passable *(road)* transitabile
   [tran-see-t*ah*-bee-lay]
passaggio a livello *grade crossing*
passenger il passeggero [pass-say-j*eh*-roh]
passerby il passante [−tay]
passport il passaporto
past: in the past in passato
   see **time**
pastry la pasta
path il sentiero [sen-tee-*eh*-roh]
patient: be patient sia paziente [s*ee*-ah
   pa-tzee-*e*n-tay]
pattern il disegno [dee-s*a*yn-yoh]

pay pagare [pa-*gah*-ray]
  can I pay, please? posso pagare, per favore?
  [. . . fa-v*oh*-ray]
peace la pace [p*ah*-chay]
peach una pesca
peanuts le arachidi [a-*rah*-kee-dee]
pear una pera [p*ay*-rah]
peas i piselli [ee . . .]
pebble il ciottolo [ch*ot*-toh-loh]
pedal il pedale [pay-d*ah*-lay]
pedestrian il pedone [pay-d*oh*-nay]
  pedestrian crossing passaggio pedonale
  [pas-s*ah*-joh pay-doh-n*ah*-lay]
» *TRAVEL TIP: do not assume that cars will stop or
  even slow down for you at a pedestrian crossing*
pedoni pedestrians
pelvis il bacino [ba-ch*ee*-noh]
pen la penna
  have you got a pen? ha una penna? [ah . . .]
pencil la matita [ma-*tee*-tah]
penpal il corrispondente [−tay]
penicillin la penicillina [pay-nee-cheel-l*ee*-nah]
penknife il temperino [-*ree*-noh]
pensioner il pensionato
people la gente [j*en*-tay]
  the Italian people gli Italiani [lee . . .]
pepper il pepe [p*ay*-pay]
  (vegetable) il peperone [−nay]
peppermint la menta [m*ay*n-tah]
per per [payr]
  per person/night/week per persona/per
  notte/per settimana
percent per cento [. . . ch*en*-toh]
perfect perfetto
  the perfect vacation la vacanza perfetta
  [va-k*an*-tzah . . .]
perfume il profumo [pro-*foo*-moh]
perhaps forse [f*or*-say]
pericolo danger
pericoloso sporgersi do not lean out

....

period il periodo [pay-*ree*-o-doh]
  (menstruation) le mestruazioni
  [mays-troo-a-tzee-*oh*-nee]
perm la permanente [−tay]
permit *(noun)* il permesso
person la persona
  in person in persona
pharmacy la farmacia [far-ma-ch*ee*-ah]
phone *see* **telephone**
photograph la fotografia [−*fee*-ah]
  would you take a photograph of us? ci fa la
  fotografia? [chee . . .]
piano il pianoforte [−tay]
pickpocket il borseggiatore [bor-say-ja-*toh*-ray]
piece il pezzo [p*e*t-tzoh]
  a piece of . . . un pezzo di . . . [. . . dee]
  a piece of that cake un pezzo di quella torta
  [p*e*t-tzoh dee . . .]
pig il maiale [ma-y*ah*-lay]
pigeon il piccione [pee-ch*oh*-nay]
pile-up un incidente a catena [een-chee-d*e*n-tay
  ah . . .]
pill la pillola [p*ee*l-lo-lah]
  do you take the pill? prendi la pillola?
pillow il cuscino [koo-sh*ee*-noh]
pin lo spillo [sp*ee*l-loh]
pineapple l'ananas
pink *(adjective)* rosa
pint la pinta [p*ee*n-tah]
» *TRAVEL TIP: 1 pint = 0.47 liters*
pipe il tubo [t*oo*-boh]
  (smoking) la pipa [p*ee*-pah]
  pipe tobacco il tabacco da pipa
piston il pistone [−nay]
pity: it's a pity è un peccato [eh . . .]
place il posto
  is this place taken? questo posto è occupato?
  do you know any good places to go?
  conosce dei posti interessanti? [ko-n*oh*-shay day
  p*o*s-tee een-tay-rays-s*a*n-tee]

plain *(food)* semplice [sem-plee-chay]
   (not patterned) senza nessun disegno [sen-tzah
   nays-soon dee-sayn-yoh]
plane l'aereo [ah-*eh*-ray-oh]
   by plane in aereo
plant la pianta [pee-*an*-tah]
plastic la plastica [pl*a*s-tee-kah]
plastic bag un sacchetto plastico
   [sak-k*a*yt-to . . .]
plate il piatto [pee-*at*-toh]
platform *(train)* il marciapiede
   [mar-cha-pee-*eh*-day]
   which platform, please? che binario, per
   favore? [kay bee-n*ah*-ree-oh payr fa-v*oh*-ray]
play: somewhere for the children to play un
   posto dove i bambini possano giocare
   [. . . d*oh*-vay ee ban-b*ee*-nee p*o*s-sa-noh
   jo-k*ah*-ray]
pleasant piacevole [pee-a-ch*a*y-vo-lay]
please per favore [payr fa-v*oh*-ray]
   could you please . . . ? potrebbe . . . ?
   [po-tr*a*yb-bay]
   yes, please sì, grazie [see gr*ah*-tzee-ay]
pleasure il piacere [pee-a-ch*a*y-ray]
   my pleasure prego [pr*ay*-goh]
plenty: plenty of . . . un sacco di . . . [. . . dee]
   thank you, that's plenty grazie, basta
   [gr*ah*-tzee-ay . . .]
pliers le pinze [p*ee*n-tzay]
plug *(electrical)* la spina [sp*ee*-nah]
   (bath) il tappo
» *TRAVEL TIP: you will need 2-pin plugs in
   Italy*
plum la prugna [pr*oo*n-yah]
plumber l'idraulico [ee-dr*ow*-lee-koh]
plus più [pew]
p.m. di pomeriggio [dee po-may-r*ee*-joh]
pneumonia la polmonite [pol-mo-n*ee*-tay]
poached egg un uovo affogato [w*o*-voh . . .]
pocket la tasca

....

point: could you point to it? me lo può
   indicare? [may lo pwoh een-dee-*kah*-ray]
   four point six quattro e sei [. . . ay say]
   points *(car)* le puntine [poon-*tee*-nay]
police la polizia [po-lee-*tzee*-ah]
   get the police chiami la polizia
   [kee-*ah*-mee . . .]
   policeman il poliziotto [po-lee-tzee-*ot*-toh]
   police station il posto di [dee] polizia
» *TRAVEL TIP: most police duties are carried out*
   by the Carabinieri; to contact the police dial
   113
polish *(noun)* il lucido [*loo*-che-doh]
   would you polish my shoes? potrebbe
   lucidarmi le scarpe? [po-*trayb*-bay
   loo-chee-*dar*-mee lay sk*ar*-pay]
polite cortese [kor-*tay*-say]
politics la politica [po-*lee*-tee-kah]
polluted inquinato [een-kwee-*nah*-toh]
pool *(swimming)* la piscina [pee-sh*ee*-nah]
poor: I'm very poor sono molto povero
   [. . . p*o*-vah-roh]
   poor quality di qualità scadente [dee
   kwa-lee-t*ah* ska-d*e*n-tay]
popular popolare [−ray]
population la popolazione [po-po-la-tzee-*oh*-nay]
pork il maiale [ma-*yah*-lay]
port *(harbor, drink)* il porto
   to port a babordo
porter il facchino [fak-k*ee*-noh]
portrait il ritratto
posh elegante [−tay]
possible possibile [pos-s*ee*-bee-lay]
   could you possibly . . . ? potrebbe . . . ?
   [po-tr*ay*b-bay]
postcard la cartolina [kar-toh-l*ee*-nah]
post office l'ufficio postale [oof-f*ee*-choh
   pos-t*ah*-lay]
   general delivery il fermo posta
» *TRAVEL TIP: postal service can be slow*
potato la patata

potato chips le patatine [pa-ta-*tee*-nay]
pottery le terraglie [ter-*ral*-yay]
pound *(weight)* la libbra [*leeb*-brah]

» *TRAVEL TIP: conversion:* $\dfrac{pounds}{11} \times 5 = kilos$

pounds	1	3	5	6	7	8	9
kilos	0.45	1.4	2.3	2.7	3.2	3.6	4.1

pour: it's pouring sta piovendo a catinelle [stah
  pee-o-*ven*-doh ah ka-tee-*nel*-lay]
powder la polvere [*pol*-vay-ray]
  (face) la cipria [*chee*-pree-ah]
power outage: there's a power outage manca
  la corrente [−tay]
prawns i gamberi [*gam*-bay-ree]
  prawn cocktail un cocktail di [dee] gamberi
prefer: I prefer this one preferisco questo
pregnant incinta [een-*cheen*-tah]
prescription la ricetta [ree-*chet*-tah]
present: at present adesso
  here's a present for you eccole un regalo
  [*ek*-ko-lay ...]
president il presidente [... *den*-tay]
press: could you press these? mi può stirare
  questi? [mee pwoh stee-*rah*-ray kwes-tee]
pretty carino [ka-*ree*-noh]
  it's pretty expensive è assai caro [eh
  as-*sah*-ee ...]
price il prezzo [*pret*-tzoh]
priest il prete [*preh*-tah]
printed matter stampe [*stam*-pay]
prison la prigione [pree-*joh*-nay]
private privato [pree-*vah*-toh]
probably probabilmente [−tay]
problem il problema
product il prodotto
profit il profitto
promise: do you promise? promette? [−tay]
  I promise prometto
**pronounce: how do you pronounce
  this?** come si pronuncia? [*koh*-may see
  pro-*noon*-chah]

pronto soccorso *first aid*
propeller l'elica [*eh*-lee-kah]
properly per bene [. . . b*a*y-nay]
prostitute una prostituta [pros-tee-*too*-tah]
protect proteggere [pro-t*eh*-jay-ray]
Protestant protestante [−t*a*n-tay]
proud orgoglioso [or-gol-y*oh*-soh]
prove: I can prove it posso provarlo
public: the public il pubblico [po*ob*-blee-koh]
  public holidays i giorni festivi [jor-nee
  fes-*tee*-vee]
» *TRAVEL TIP: public holidays: January 1st*
  ("Capodanno"); Good Friday ("Venerdì Santo");
  Easter Monday ("Pasqua"); April 25th; May 1st;
  August 15th ("l'Assunzione"); November 1st
  ("Ognissanti"); December 8th ("l'Immacolata
  Concezione"); December 25th ("Natale");
  December 26th ("Santo Stefano")
pudding il budino [boo-d*ee*-noh]
  (dessert) il dolce [dol-chay]
pull *(verb)* tirare [tee-r*ah*-ray]
  he pulled out in front of me mi ha tagliato
  la strada [mee ah tal-y*ah*-toh la str*ah*-dah]
pump la pompa
punctual puntuale [poon-too-*ah*-lay]
puncture una foratura [fo-ra-*too*-rah]
pure puro [p*oo*-roh]
purple porpora [p*o*r-po-rah]
purse il borsello
push *(verb)* spingere [sp*ee*n-jay-ray]
put: where can I put . . . ? dove posso
  mettere . . . ? [d*o*h-vay pos-soh met-tay-ray]
quality la qualità [kwa-lee-t*ah*]
quarantine la quarantena [kwa-ran-t*ay*-nah]
quarter un quarto [kw*a*r-toh]
  a quarter of an hour un quarto d'ora
  see **time**
quay il molo
question una domanda
quick svelto

that was quick è stato svelto [eh st*a*h-toh . . .]
quiet quieto [kwee-*ay*-toh]
   be quiet! zitto! [tz*ee*t-toh]
quite completamente [−tay]
   (fairly) assai [as-s*a*h-ee]
   quite a lot un sacco
race *(auto, etc.)* una corsa
radiator il radiatore [ra-dee-a-t*oh*-ray]
radio la radio [r*a*h-dee-oh]
rail: by rail col treno
rain la pioggia [pee-*o*-jah]
   it's raining piove [pee-*o*-vay]
   raincoat l'impermeabile
   [eem-per-may-*a*h-bee-lay]
rallentare slow down
rally *(car)* il rally
rape lo stupro [st*oo*-proh]
rare raro; *(steak)* al sangue [. . . san-gway]
raspberry il lampone [lam-p*oh*-nay]
rat un ratto
rather: I'd rather sit here preferisco sedere qui
   [. . . say-d*ay*-ray kwee]
   I'd rather not preferisco di [dee] no
   it's rather hot fa piuttosto caldo
   [. . . pewt-t*os*-toh . . .]
raw crudo [kr*oo*-doh]
razor rasoio [ra-s*oh*-yoh]
   razor blades le lamette da barba
   [la-m*a*yt-tay . . .]
read: would you read it for me? me lo può
   leggere? [may loh pwoh l*eh*-jay-ray]
   something to read qualcosa da leggere
ready: when will it be ready? per quando è
   pronto? [. . . eh . . .]
   I'm not ready yet non sono ancora pronto
real autentico [ow-t*e*n-tee-koh]
   real leather vera pelle [v*ay*-rah p*e*l-lay]
   (shoes) vero cuoio [. . . kw*o*-yoh]
   it's a real bargain è un vero affare [eh . . .
   af-f*a*h-ray]

really davvero [dav-vay-roh]

rearview mirror lo specchietto retrovisore
[spayk-yet-toh ray-tro-vee-soh-ray]

reasonable ragionevole [ra-jo-nay-vo-lay]

receipt la ricevuta [ree-chay-voo-tah]

   can I have a receipt, please posso avere la
ricevuta, per favore? [pos-soh a-vay-ray ... payr
fa-voh-ray]

recently di recente [dee ray-chen-tay]

reception *(hotel)* il ricevimento [ree-chay
vee-men-toh]

   at the reception desk al ricevimento

recipe la ricetta [ree-chet-tah]

recommend: can you recommend ... ? può
consigliare ... ? [pwoh kon-seel-yah-ray]

record *(music)* un disco [dees-koh]

red rosso

reduction *(in price)* uno sconto

refuse: I refuse mi rifiuto [mee ree-few-toh]

refrigerator il frigo [free-goh]

region la regione [ray-joh-nay]

registered letter una lettera raccomandata
[let-tay-rah ...]

regret: I regret that ... mi rincresce che ...
[mee reen-kray-shay kay]

relax: I just want to relax voglio riposarmi
[vol-yoh ree-po-sar-mee]

remember: don't you remember? non si [see]
ricorda?

   I'll always remember mi ricorderò sempre
[mee ree-kor-day-ro sem-pray]

   something to remember you by qualcosa
per ricordarti

rent: can I rent a car/boat/bicycle? posso
affittare una macchina/barca/bicicletta?
[... af-feet-tah-ray oo-nah mak-kee-nah/
bar-kah/bee-chee-klayt-tah]

repair: can you repair it? può ripararlo?
[pwoh ...]

repeat: could you repeat that? può ripetere?
[pwoh ree-peh-tay-ray]

reputation la reputazione
[ray-poo-ta-tzee-*oh*-nay]
rescue *(verb)* salvare [−ray]
reservation la prenotazione
[pray-no-ta-tzee-*oh*-nay]
   I want to make a reservation for . . . vorrei
   fare una prenotazione per . . . [vor-*ray*
   f*ah*-ray . . .]
reserve: can I reserve a seat? posso prenotare
   un posto? [. . . pray-no-t*ah*-ray . . .]
   I'd like to reserve a table for two vorrei
   prenotare un tavolo per due [vor-*ray* pray-not-
   ah-ray oon t*ah*-vo-lo payr d*oo*-ay]
responsible responsabile [res-pon-s*ah*-bee-lay]
rest: I've come here for a rest sono venuto qua
   per riposarmi
   you keep the rest tenga il resto
rest room la toilette [twa-let]
   where is the rest room? dove sono le
   toilette? [d*oh*-vay s*oh*-noh lay twa-let]
   public restroom la toilette
   » *TRAVEL TIP: see* **toilet**
restaurant il ristorante [−tay]
retail price il prezzo al minuto [pr*et*-tzoh . . .]
retired in pensione [een payn-see-*oh*-nay]
reverse gear la marcia indietro [m*ar*-chah
   een-dee-*eh*-troh]
rheumatism il reumatismo [ray-oo-ma-t*ees*-moh]
rib la costola [k*os*-toh-lah]
rice il riso [*ree*-soh]
rich ricco [r*eek*-koh]
ridiculous ridicolo [ree-d*ee*-ko-loh]
right: that's right è vero [eh-v*ay*-roh]
   you're right ha ragione lei [ah-ra-j*oh*-nay lay]
   on the right a destra
   right now proprio adesso [pro-pree-oh . . .]
   (immediately) subito
   right here proprio qui [pro-pree-oh kwee]
   right-hand drive la guida a destra [gw*ee*-dah
   ah . . .]
ring *(on finger)* l'anello

ripe maturo [mat-*too*-roh]

rip-off: it's a rip-off è un furto [eh oon *foo*r-toh]

riservato *reserved*

river il fiume [*few*-may]

road la strada

    which is the road to...? qual'è la strada
per...? [kwa-l*eh*...]

    roadhog un guidatore incosciente
[gwee-da-t*oh*-ray een-ko-sh*en*-tay]

rob: I've been robbed sono stato derubato

rock la roccia [*ro*-chah]

    whisky on the rocks un whisky con ghiaccio
[ghee-*ah*-choh]

roll *(bread)* un panino [pa-n*ee*-noh]

Roman Catholic cattolico [kat-*toh*-lee-koh]

romantic romantico [ro-m*an*-tee-koh]

roof il tetto

room la camera [*kah*-may-rah]

    have you got a (single/double) room? ha
una camera (singola/doppia)? [ah...
s*ee*n-go-lah/dop-pee-ah]

    for one night/for three nights per una
notte/per tre notti [...n*o*t-tay]

    YOU MAY THEN HEAR...

    con doccia *with shower*

    con bagno *with bath*

    spiacenti, ma ciamo al completo *sorry, we're
full*

room service il servizio [ser-v*ee*-tzee-oh]

rope la fune [*foo*-nay]

rose la rosa

rosé rosé

rough *(sea)* agitato

roughly *(approximately)* più o meno [pew o
m*ay*-noh]

roulette la roulette

round *(circular)* rotondo

roundabout la rotonda

» *TRAVEL TIP: cars on the roundabout must give
way to traffic joining the roundabout*

**round-trip: a round-trip ticket
   to...** un'andata e [ay] ritorno per...
**route: which is the prettiest/fastest
   route?** qual'è la strada più bella/più veloce?
   [kwa-leh lah strah-dah pew bel-lah/pew
   vay-loh-chay]
rowboat una barca a remi [... ray-mee]
rubber la gomma
   rubber band un elastico [ay-las-tee-koh]
rudder il timone [tee-moh-nay]
rude maleducato [ma-lay-doo-kah-toh]
ruins le rovine [ro-vee-nay]
rum il rum [room]
   rum and Coke un rum e coca-cola
   [... ay ...]
run: hurry, run! corri, fa presto!
   I've run out of gas/money sono rimasto
   senza benzina/soldi [... sen-tzah
   ben-tzee-nah/sol-dee]
sad triste [trees-tay]
safe sicuro [see-koo-roh]
   will it be safe here? è al sicuro qua? [eh ...]
   is it safe to swim here? è prudente nuotare
   qua? [−tay nwo-tah-ray ...]
safety la sicurezza [see-koo-rayt-tzah]
   safety pin la spilla di sicurezza [speel-lah
   dee ...]
sail le vela [vay-lah]
   can we go sailing? possiamo fare [fah-ray]
   della barca a vela?
sailor il marinaio [ma-ree-nah-yoh]
sala d'aspetto waiting room
salad l'insalata
salami il salame [−may]
saldi sale
sale: is it for sale? è in vendita [eh een
   vayn-dee-tah]
salesclerk la commessa
salmon il salmone [sal-moh-nay]
salt il sale [sah-lay]

same stesso
 the same again, please ancora dello stesso,
 per favore [. . . fa-voh-ray]
 the same to you altrettanto
sand la sabbia
sandal il sandalo [san-da-loh]
sandwich un panino imbottito [pa-nee-noh
 eem-bot-tee-toh]
sanitary napkins gli assorbenti igienici
 [lee . . . ee-jay-nee-chee]
Sardinia la Sardegna [sar-dayn-yah]
satisfactory soddisfacente [sod-dees-fa-chen-tay]
Saturday sabato [sah-ba-toh]
sauce la salsa
 saucepan la casseruola [kas-sayr-wo-lah]
saucer il piattino [pee-at-tee-noh]
sauna la sauna [sah-oo-nah]
sausage la salsiccia [sal-see-chah]
save *(life)* salvare [sal-vah-ray]
say: how do you say . . . in Italian? come si
 dice in italiano . . . ? [koh-may see dee-chay . . .]
 what did he say? cosa ha detto? [. . . ha . . .]
scala mobile escalator
scarf il fazzoletto [fat-tzo-layt-toh]
scenery il panorama
schedule il programma
 on/behind schedule in orario/in ritardo
 scheduled flight il volo di linea [. . . dee
 lee-nay-ah]
school la scuola [skwo-lah]
scissors: a pair of scissors un paio di forbici
 [pah-yoh dee for-bee-chee]
scooter il motorino [mo-to-ree-noh]
Scotland la Scozia [sko-tzee-ah]
Scottish scozzese [skot-tzay-say]
scrambled eggs le uova strapazzate [lay wo-vah
 stra-pat-tzah-tay]
scratch un graffio [graf-fee-oh]
scream un grido [gree-doh]
screw *(noun)* la vite [vee-tay]
 screwdriver il cacciavite [ka-cha-vee-tay]

....

sea il mare [m*ah*-ray]
  by the sea al mare
seafood i frutti di mare [ee fr*oo*t-tee dee
  m*ah*-ray]
search cercare [chayr-k*ah*-ray]
  search party squadra il soccorso [skw*ah*-drah
  dee . . .]
seasick: I get seasick soffro il mal di mare
  [. . . dee m*ah*-ray]
  I feel seasick ho mal di mare [o . . .]
season la stagione [sta-j*oh*-nay]
  in the high/low season in alta/bassa
  stagione
seasoning il condimento
seat un posto a sedere [. . . say-d*ay*-ray]
  is this somebody's seat? è occupato questo
  posto?
  seat belt la cintura di sicurezza [cheen-t*oo*-rah
  dee see-koo-r*ay*t-tzah]
seaweed le alghe [*al*-gay]
second secondo
  just a second un secondo
  secondhand di seconda mano [dee . . .]
secret: it's a secret è un segreto [eh . . .]
see vedere [vay-d*ay*-ray]
  I see *(understand)* ho capito [o ka-p*ee*-toh]
  have you seen . . . ? ha visto . . . ? [ah . . .]
  can I see the room? posso vedere la camera?
seem sembrare [saym-br*ah*-ray]
  it seems so pare di si [p*ah*-ray dee see]
seldom raramente [ra-ra-m*en*-tay]
self: self-service il self-service
sell vendere [v*ay*n-day-ray]
send spedire [spay-d*ee*-ray]
sensitive sensibile [sen-s*ee*-bee-lay]
sentimental sentimentale [−t*ah*-lay]
separate *(adjective)* separato [say-pa-r*ah*-toh]
  I'm separated sono diviso [. . . dee-v*ee*-soh]
  can we pay separately? possiamo avere conti
  separati? [. . . a-v*ay*-ray . . .]
September settembre [−bray]

....

serious serio [*seh*-ree-oh]
  I'm serious sul serio
  this is serious questo è grave [. . . gr*ah*-vay]
  is it serious, doctor? è grave, dottore?
service: the service was excellent/poor il
  servizio era eccellente/lasciava a desiderare
  [ser-*vee*-tzee-oh *eh*-rah ay-chayl-l*en*-tay/la-sh*ah*-
  vah ah day-see-day-r*ah*-ray]
service station la stazione de servizio
  [sta-tzee-*oh*-nay dee . . .]
several diversi [dee-v*er*-see]
sexy sexy
shade: in the shade all'ombra
shake scuotere [skw*o*-tay-ray]
  to shake hands stringere la mano
  [str*ee*n-jay-ray lah m*ah*-noh]
» *TRAVEL TIP: customary to shake hands each time*
  you meet somebody and when you take your
  leave of somebody
shallow basso
shame: what a shame! che peccato! [kay . . .]
shampoo *(noun)* lo shampoo [sh*am*-poh]
  shampoo and set shampoo e messa in piega
  [. . . pee-*ay*-gah]
share *(room, table)* dividere [dee-v*ee*-day-ray]
shark lo squalo [skw*ah*-loh]
sharp *(pain)* acuto [a-k*oo*-toh]
  (blade) affilato
  (taste) acido [*ah*-chee-doh]
  (bend) stretto
shave radersi [r*ah*-dayr-see]
  shaver un rasoio [ra-s*oh*-yoh]
  shaving cream schiuma da barba
  [sk*ew*-mah . . .]
she lei [lay]
  she is è [eh]
sheep la pecora [p*eh*-ko-rah]
sheet il lenzuolo [len-tzw*o*-loh]
  you haven't changed my sheets non avete
  cambiato le lenzuola [non a-v*ay*-tay
  kam-bee-*ah*-toh lay layn-tzw*o*-lah]

shelf lo scaffale [skaf-*fah*-lay]
shell la conchiglia [kon-*kee*l-yah]
  shellfish i molluschi [ee mol-*loos*-kee]
shelter *(noun)* un riparo
sherry lo sherry
shin la tibia [*tee*-bee-ah]
ship la nave [*nah*-vay]
  by ship con la nave
shirt la camicia [ka-m*ee*-chah]
shock *(noun: surprise)* lo shock
  I got an electric shock from the... ho
  preso la scossa con... [o...]
  shock absorber l'ammortizzatore
  [am-mor-teet-tza-t*oh*-ray]
shoe la scarpa
» *TRAVEL TIP: women's shoe sizes*

US	5	6	7	8	9	10
Italy	36	37	38	39	40	41

men's shoe sizes

US	7	8	9	10	11	12
Italy	39½	41	42	43	44½	46

shop il negozio [nay-go-tzee-oh]
  I have some shopping to do devo fare delle
  compere [d*ay*-voh f*ah*-ray d*el*-lay kom-p*ay*-ray]
» *TRAVEL TIP: shops usually close for lunch*
  between 12:30 and 3:30 in winter, 12:30 and
  4:30 in summer, and remain open till 7 or
  8 p.m.
shore la costa
  on the shore sulla spiaggia [s*oo*l-lah
  spee-*ah*-jah]
short corto
  I'm three short me ne mancano tre [may nay
  m*a*n-ka-noh tray]
  short cut la scorciatoia [skor-cha-t*oh*-yah]
shorts i calzoncini [ee kal-tzon-ch*ee*-nee]
shoulder la spalla
shout *(verb)* gridare [gree-d*ah*-ray]
show: please show me mi può mostrare? [mee
  pwoh mos-tr*ah*-ray]

....

shower: with shower con doccia [d*oh*-chah]
shrimp i gamberetti
shrink: it's shrunk si è ristretto [see ...]
shut *(verb)* chiudere [kee-*oo*-day-ray]
   shut up! sta'zitto! [stah-tz*eet*-toh]
shy timido [t*ee*-mee-doh]
si prega di non... please do not...
Sicily la Sicilia [see-ch*ee*l-yah]
sick malato [ma-l*ah*-toh]
   I feel sick mi sento male [mee s*e*n-toh
   m*ah*-lay]
   he's been sick è stato male [eh st*ah*-toh ...]
side il lato [l*ah*-toh]
   side street una laterale [−lay]
   by the side of the road sul margine della
   strada [sool mar-jee-nay ...]
sidewalk il marciapiede [mar-cha-pee-*eh*-day]
sight: out of sight fuori vista [fw*oh*-ree
   v*ee*s-tah]
   **we'd like to go on a sightseeing
   tour** vorremmo fare una gita turistica
   [... f*ah*-ray *oo*-nah j*ee*-tah too-r*ee*s-tee-kah]
sign *(notice)* il cartello
signal: he didn't signal non ha indicato [non ah
   een-dee-k*ah*-toh]
signature la firma
signore ladies' restroom
signori gentlemen's restroom
silence *(noun)* il silenzio [see-l*e*n-tzee-oh]
silk la seta [s*ay*-tah]
silly sciocco [sh*o*k-koh]
silver l'argento [ar-j*e*n-toh]
similar simile [s*ee*-mee-lay]
simple semplice [s*ay*m-plee-chay]
since: since last week dalla settimana scorsa
   since we arrived da quando siamo arrivati
   (because) poiché [poy-k*ay*]
sincere sincero [seen-ch*ay*-roh]
   yours sincerely cordiali saluti
sing cantare [kan-t*ah*-ray]

....

single: single room una camera singola
[k*a*h-may-rah s*ee*n-go-lah]
  I'm single non sono sposato
sink: it sank è affondato
sir signore [seen-y*o*h-ray]
sister: my sister mia sorella [m*ee*-ah . . .]
sit: can I sit here? posso sedermi qui?
  [. . . say-d*a*yr-mee kwee]
size *(clothes)* la taglia [t*a*l-yah]
  (shoes) il numero [n*oo*-may-roh]
ski *(noun)* lo sci [shee]
  (verb) sciare [shee-*a*h-ray]
  skiing lo sciare
  ski boots gli scarponi da sci [lee skar-p*o*h-nee
  dah shee]
  ski lift la sciovia [shee-o-v*ee*-ah]
  ski pants i pantaloni da sci
  [pan-ta-l*o*h-nee . . .]
  ski pole la racchetta de sci [rak-k*a*yt-tah . . .]
  ski slope/ski run la pista da sci
  [p*ee*s-tah . . .]
  ski wax la sciolina [shee-o-l*ee*-nah]
skid sbandare [sban-d*a*h-ray]
skin la pelle [pel-lay]
  skin diving il nuoto subacqueo [nw*o*-toh soo-
  b*a*h-kway-oh]
skirt la gonna
sky il cielo [ch*a*y-loh]
  in the sky in cielo
sled la slitta
sleep: I can't sleep non riesco a dormire
  [. . . ree-*a*ys-koh ah dor-m*ee*-ray]
  sleeper *(rail)* il vagone letto [va-g*o*h-nay . . .]
  sleeping bag il sacco a pelo
  sleeping pill un sonnifero [sonn-n*ee*-fay-roh]
  YOU MAY HEAR . . .
  ha dormito bene? *did you sleep well?*
sleeve la manica [m*a*h-nee-kah]
slide *(photographic)* una diapositiva
  [dee-a-po-see-t*ee*-vah]

slow: could you speak a little slower? può parlare un po' più lentamente? [pwoh par-*lah*-ray oon po pew len-ta-m*ay*n-tay]

small piccolo

    small change la moneta [mo-n*ay*-tah]

smell: there's a funny smell c'è un odore strano [chay oon o-d*oh*-ray . . .]

    it smells puzza [p*oo*t-tzah]

smile *(verb)* sorridere [sor-ree-day-ray]

smoke *(noun)* il fumo [*foo*-moh]

    do you smoke? fuma?

    can I smoke? posso fumare? [. . . foo-m*ah*-ray]

smooth liscio [*lee*-shoh]

snack spuntino [spoon-*tee*-noh]

    can we just have a snack? non vorremmo un pasto completo

snake una serpe [–pay]

snorkel un respiratore [–t*oh*-ray]

snow *(noun)* la neve [n*ay*-vay]

so: it's so hot fa così caldo [. . . ko-s*ee* . . .]

    not so much non così tanto

    so-so così-così

soap il sapone [sa-p*oh*-nay]

sober non ubriaco [. . . oo-bree-*ah*-koh]

socks i calzini [kal-tz*ee*-nee]

soda water l'acqua di [dee] soda

soft drink un analcolico [a-nal-ko-lee-koh]

sole *(shoe)* la suola [sw*oh*-lah]

    could you put new soles on these? può risuolarmi queste? [pwoh ree-swo-l*ar*-mee kwes-tay]

YOU MAY THEN HEAR . . .

di cuoio o di gomma? *leather or rubber?*

some: some people alcune persone [al-k*oo*-nay per-s*oh*-nay]

    can I have some? posso averne un po'? [. . . a-v*ay*r-nay . . .]

    can I have some grapes/some bread? posso avere dell'uva/del pane? [. . . a-v*ay*-ray del-*loo*-vah/del p*ah*-nay]

can I have some more? posso averne ancora
[. . . a-*vayr*-nay . . .]
somebody qualcuno [kwal-*koo*-noh]
something qualcosa
sometimes a volte [ah vol-tay]
somewhere da qualche parte [. . . kw*al*-kay
p*ar*-tay]
son: my son mio figlio [m*ee*-oh f*eel*-yoh]
song una canzone [kan-tz*oh*-nay]
soon presto
  as soon as possible appena possibile
  [. . . pos-s*ee*-bee-lay]
  sooner prima [pr*ee*-mah]
sore: it's sore mi fa male [mee fah m*ah*-lay]
  sore throat il mal di gola [. . . dee . . .]
sorry: (I'm) sorry mi spiace [mee spee-*ah*-chay]
sort: this sort questo tipo [. . . t*ee*-poh]
  will you sort it out? ci pensa lei? [chee
  p*en*-sah lay]
sosta autorizzata (9-12) parking (between 9 and
  12)
sosta vietata no waiting
sottopassaggio underpass
soup la zuppa [tz*oop*-pah]
sought sud [sood]
South Africa il Sudafrica [soo-d*ah*-free-kah]
South African sudafricano
souvenir un souvenir
spade la vanga
  (child's) la paletta
spaghetti gli spaghetti [lee spa-g*ayt*-tee]
spare: spare part il pezzo di ricambio [pet-tzoh
  dee ree-k*am*-bee-oh]
  spare wheel la ruota di scorta [rwo-tah
  dee . . .]
spark plug la candela
speak: do you speak English? parla l'inglese?
  [. . . leen-gl*ay*-say]
  I don't speak Italian non parlo l'italiano
special speciale [spay-ch*ah*-lay]

specialist lo specialista [spay-chal-*lees*-tah]
specially specialmente [spay-chal-*mayn*-tay]
speed la velocità [vay-lo-chee-*tah*]
   he was speeding aveva superato il limite di
   velocità [. . . *lee*-mee-tay dee . . .]
   speed limit il limite de velocità
   speedometer il tachimetro [ta-*kee*-may-troh]
spend *(money)* spendere [spen-*day*-ray]
spices le spezie [spet-zee-ay]
   is it spicy? è piccante? [eh peek-*kan*-tay]
   it's too spicy è troppo piccante
spider il ragno [*ran*-yoh]
spingere push
spirits le bevande alcoliche [lay bay-*van*-day
   al-ko-*lee*-kay]
spoon il cucchiaio [kook-*yah*-yoh]
sprain *(noun)* una storta
   I've sprained my ankle ho preso una storta
   alla caviglia [o . . . ka *veel*-yah]
spring la molla
   (season) la primavera [pree-ma-*veh*-rah]
square *(in town)* la piazza [pee-*at*-tzah]
   two square meters due metri quadri [*doo*-ay . . .]
stairs le scale [lay s*kah*-lay]
stake *(tent)* il picchetto [peek-*kayt*-toh]
stall: it keeps stalling non fa altro che fermarsi
   [. . . *kay* . . .]
stalls *(theater)* la platea [pla-*teh*-ah]
stamp il francobollo [fran-ko-*bol*-loh]
   two stamps for the United States, please
   due francobolli per gli Stati Uniti, per favore
   [*doo*-ay . . . payr lee s*tah*-tee oo-*nee*-tee, payr
   fa-*voh*-ray]
» *TRAVEL TIP: buy stamps at tobacconists and*
   most bars
stand *(verb)* stare in piedi [s*tah*-ray een
   pee-*eh*-dee]
   (at fair) lo stand
standard *(adjective)* medio [med-*yoh*]
   standard model un modello standard

....

stand-by de riserva [dee . . .]
star una stella
starboard tribordo [tree-bor-doh]
start: my car won't start la macchina non
    parte [mak-kee-nah non par-tay]
    when does it start? quando comincia?
    [kwan-doh ko-meen-chah]
starter *(car)* il motorino d'avviamento
    [mo-to-ree-noh dav-vee-a-mayn-toh]
starving: I'm starving sto morendo di fame
    [. . . dee fah-may]
station la stazione [sta-tzee-oh-nay]
statue la statua [stah-too-ah]
stay: can we stay here? possiamo ripararci
    qua?
    we enjoyed our stay abbiamo avuto un
    soggiorno piacevole [ab-bee-ah-moh a-voo-toh
    oon so-jor-noh pee-a-chay-vo-lay]
    stay there resta lì [. . . lee]
    I'm staying at . . . sono al . . .
steak la bistecca [bees-tayk-kah]
    YOU MAY THEN HEAR . . .
    al sangue [al san-gway] *rare*
    poco cotta *medium rare*
    cotta bene [. . . bay-nay] *well done*
steep ripido [ree-pee-doh]
steering *(car)* lo sterzo [stayr-tzoh]
steering wheel il volante [−tay]
step *(stairs)* il gradino [gra-dee-noh]
stereo stereo
stewardess la hostess
sticky appiccicoso [ap-pee-chee-koh-soh]
stiff rigido [ree-jee-doh]
still *(adjective)* calmo [kal-mo]
    keep still sta'fermo
    I'm still here sono ancora qui
stink *(noun)* una puzza [poot-tzah]
stolen: my wallet's been stolen mi hanno
    rubato il portafoglio [mee-an-noh roo-bah-toh
    eel por-ta-fol-yoh]

....

stomach lo stomaco [sto-ma-koh]
  I've got a stomachache ho il mal di stomaco
  [o eel mal dee . . .]
  **have you got something for an upset
  stomach?** ha qualcosa per il mal di stomaco?
  [ah . . .]
stone la pietra [pee-eh-trah]
stop: stop! ferma!
  stopover la fermata
  do you stop near . . . ? si ferma vicino . . . ?
  [see fer-mah vee-chee-noh ah]
storm il temporale [taym-po-rah-lay]
stove la cucina [koo-chee-nah]
straight diritto [dee-reet-toh]
  go straight on sempre diritto [sem-pray . . .]
  straight whisky un whisky liscio [lee-shoh]
strange strano
stranger un estraneo [es-trah-nay-oh]
  I'm a stranger here non sono pratico del
  luogo [. . . prah-tee-koh del lwo-goh]
strawberry la fragola [frah-go-lah]
street la strada
string: have you got any string? ha della
  corda? [ah . . .]
striptease lo striptease
stroke: he's had a stroke gli è venuto un
  attacco [lee eh vay-noo-toh . . .]
stroller il passeggino [pas-say-jee-noh]
strong forte [for-tay]
student uno studente [stoo-den-tay]
stung: I've been stung sono stato punto
  [. . . poon-toh]
stupid stupido [stoo-pee-doh]
such: such a lot così tanto [ko-see . . .]
suddenly improvvisamente [−tay]
sugar lo zucchero [tzoo-kay-roh]
suit (man's) l'abito [ah-bee-toh]
  (woman's) il tailleur [ta-yoor]
  suitcase una valigia [va-lee-jah]
suitable adatto
summer l'estate [es-tah-tay]

sun il sole [*soh*-lay]
  in the sun al sole
  out of the sun all'ombra
  sunbathe prendere il sole [pren-day-ray . . .]
  sunburn la scottatura [skot-ta-*too*-rah]
  sunglasses gli occhiali da sole [lee ok-*yah*-lee . . .]
  suntan oil l'olio solare [*lol*-yoh so-*lah*-ray]
  sunstroke il colpo di [dee] sole
Sunday domenica [doh-*may*-nee-kah]
suonare *please ring*
supermarket il supermercato
sure: I'm not sure non sono sicuro [see-*koo*-roh]
  sure! certamente! [chayr-ta-*mayn*-tay]
  are you sure? è sicuro? [eh . . .]
surfboard la tavola da surfing
surfing: to go surfing andare a fare il surfing [an-*dar*-ray ah *fah*-ray eel . . .]
surname il cognome [kon-*yoh*-may]
swearword una parolaccia [pa-ro-*lah*-chah]
sweat *(verb)* sudare [soo-*dah*-ray]
sweater un maglione [mal-*yoh*-nay]
sweet: it's too sweet è troppo dolce [eh . . . *dol*-chay]
sweets caramelle [−lay]
swerve: I had to swerve ho dovuto deviare improvvisamente [o do-*voo*-toh day-vee-*ah*-ray eem-prov-vee-sa-men-tay]
swim: I'm going for a swim vado a fare una nuotata [*vah*-doh ah *fah*-ray *oo*-nah nwo-*tah*-tah]
  swimsuit il costume da bagno [kos-*too*-may dah ban-yoh]
  swimming pool la piscina [pee-sh*ee*-nah]
Swiss svizzero [sv*ee*t-tzay-roh]
switch *(noun)* l'interruttore [een-ter-root-*toh*-ray]
  to switch (something) on/off accendere/spegnere (qualcosa) [a-ch*e*n-day-ray/ spen-yay-ray . . .]
Switzerland la Svizzera [sv*ee*t-tzay-rah]

....

table la tavola [*tah*-vo-lah]
   a table for 4 un tavolo per quattro
   table wine un vino da pasto [*vee*-noh . . .]
take prendere [pr*e*n-day-ray]
   can I take this with me? posso prendere
   questo?
   will you take me to the airport? mi può
   condurre all'aeroporto? [mee pwoh kon-d*oo*r-ray
   al-la-ay-ro-p*o*r-toh]
   how long will it take? quanto ci vorrà?
   [. . . chee . . .]
   somebody has taken my bags qualcuno ha
   preso le mie valigie [. . . ah pr*ay*-soh lay m*ee*-ay
   va-*lee*-jay]
   can I take you out tonight? posso portarti
   fuori questa sera? [. . . fw*oh*-ree . . .]
   is this seat taken? è occupato? [eh . . .]
talcum powder il borotalco
talk *(verb)* parlare [par-l*ah*-ray]
tall alto
tampons i tamponi [ee tam-p*oh*-nee]
tan l'abbronzatura [ab-bron-tza-*too*-rah]
   I want to get a tan voglio abbronzarmi
   [v*o*l-yoh ab-bron-tz*ar*-mee]
tank *(of car)* il serbatoio [sayr-ba-t*oh*-yoh]
tape il nastro
tape recorder il registratore [ray-jees-tra-
   toh-ray]
tariff la tariffa
taste *(noun) (food)* il sapore [sa-p*oh*-ray]
   (clothes, etc.) il gusto [g*oo*s-toh]
   can I taste it? posso assaggiare?
   [as-sa-j*ah*-ray]
   it tastes horrible/very nice fa schifo/è molto
   buono [fah sk*ee*-foh/eh m*o*l-toh bw*o*-noh]
taxi il tassì [tas-s*ee*]
   will you get me a taxi? mi può chiamare un
   tassì? [mee pwoh kee-a-m*ah*-ray . . .]
   where can I get a taxi? dove posso prendere
   un tassì? [d*oh*-vay p*o*s-soh pr*e*n-day-ray . . .]
   taxi driver il tassista

tea il tè [teh]
   could I have some tea? posso avere un tè?
   [. . . a-v*ay*-ray . . .]
   tea with milk/with lemon tè al latte/al
   limone [. . . l*at*-tay/al lee-m*oh*-nay]
   teapot una teiera [tay-yeh-rah]
  » *TRAVEL TIP: tea is usually served either black or*
    with lemon ("al limone"); tea with milk is very
    unusual and milk must be ordered separately
teach: could you teach me? mi può insegnare?
   [mee pwoh een-sayn-y*ah*-ray]
teacher l'insegnante [een-sayn-y*an*-tay]
telegram il telegramma
   I want to send a telegram vorrei spedire un
   telegramma [vor-r*ay* spay-d*ee*-ray . . .]
telephone *(noun)* il telefono [tay-l*eh*-fo-noh]
   telephone booth un telefono pubblico
   [tay-l*eh*-fo-noh p*oo*b-blee-koh]
   can I make a phonecall? posso fare una
   telefonata? [. . . f*ah*-ray . . .]
   can I speak to . . . ? posso parlare con . . . ?
   [. . . par-l*ah*-ray . . .]
   could you get this number for me? mi può
   chiamare questo numero? [mee pwoh
   kee-ah-m*ah*-ray kwes-toh n*oo*-may-roh]
   telephone directory l'elenco telefonico
   [. . . tay-lay-fo-nee-koh]
  » *TRAVEL TIP: for public phones you'll need tokens*
    (gettoni), 1 for local, min. of 6 for international
    calls; buy gettoni at tobacconists, bars, post
    offices, newsstands; code for US is 001; in
    larger towns go to SIP where the assistant will
    put you through
television la televisione [tay-lay-vee-see-*oh*-nay]
   I'd like to watch television vorrei guardare
   la televisione [vor-r*ay* gwar-d*ah*-ray . . .]
tell: could you tell me where . . . ? mi può dire
   dove . . . ? [mee pwoh d*ee*-ray d*oh*-vay]
temperature *(weather etc.)* la temperatura
   [–t*oo*-rah]
temporary temporaneo [–r*ah*-nay-oh]

....

tenere la destra *keep right*
tennis il tennis
   tennis court il campo da tennis
   tennis racket la racchetta da tennis
   [rak-*kayt*-tah . . .]
   tennis ball la palla da tennis
tent la tenda
terminal il capolinea [ka-po-*lee*-nay-ah]
terrible terribile [ter-*ree*-bee-lay]
terrific magnifico [man-*yee*-fee-koh]
than di [dee]
   bigger/older than . . . più grande/più vecchio
   di . . . [pew gr*a*n-day/pew vek-yoh dee]
thanks, thank you grazie [*grah*-tzee-ay]
   no thank you no grazie
   thank you very much grazie tante
   [. . . t*a*n-tay]
   thank you for your help grazie per l'aiuto
   YOU MAY THEN HEAR . . .
   prego *you're welcome*
that quello
   that man/that table quell'uomo/quella tavola
   [kwayl-w*o*-moh/kw*a*yl-t*a*h-vo-lah]
   I would like that one vorrei quello
   [vor-*ray* . . .]
   how do you say that? come si dice? [*koh*-may
   see d*ee*-chay]
the *(singular)* il, lo; la
   (plural) i [ee]; gli [lee]; le [lay]
theater il teatro [tay-*ah*-troh]
their il loro; la loro
   it's their bag/it's theirs è la loro borsa/è loro
them loro
   I see them li vedo [lee v*ay*-doh]
then allora
there lì [lee]
   how do I get there? come ci arrivo? [*koh*-may
   chee ar-*ree*-voh]
   is there . . . /are there . . . ? c'è . . . /ci sono . . . ?
   [cheh . . . /chee s*oh*-noh]
   there you are *(giving something)* ecco

....

thermos bottle il thermos [t*a*yr-mos]
these questi
  these apples queste mele [. . . m*a*y-lay]
  can I take these? posso prendere questi?
  [. . . pren-day-ray . . .]
they essi [*es*-see]
  they are sono
thick spesso
thief il ladro
thigh la coscia [k*oh*-shah]
thin sottile [sot-*tee*-lay]
thing una cosa
  I've lost all my things ho perso tutto quello
  che avevo [o p*e*r-soh t*oot*-toh kw*a*yl-loh kay
  a-v*a*y-voh]
think pensare [pen-s*ah*-ray]
  I'll think it over ci penso su [chee . . . soo]
  I think so/I don't think so penso di sì/di no
  [pen-soh dee see . . .]
third *(adjective)* terzo [t*a*yr-tzoh]
thirsty: I'm thirsty ho sete [o s*a*y-tay]
this questo
  this hotel/this street quest'albergo/questa
  strada
  can I have this one? posso avere questo?
  this is my wife/this is Mr. . . . questa è mia
  moglie/questo è il signor . . . [. . . m*ee*-ah
  m*o*l-yah . . . /eel seen-yor . . .]
  is this . . . ? è questo . . . [eh . . .]
those quelli; quelle [kw*a*yl-lee kw*a*yl-lay]
  how much are those? quanto costano?
  [. . . k*o*s-ta-noh]
thousand mille [m*ee*l-lay]
  thousands migliaia [meel-y*ah*-yah]
thread *(noun)* il filo [f*ee*-loh]
three tre [tray]
throat la gola [g*oh*-lah]
throttle l'acceleratore [a-chay-lay-ra-t*oh*-ray]
through attraverso
  through there per di là [. . . dee lah]
throw *(verb)* gettare [jet-t*ah*-ray]

....

thumb il pollice [p*o*l-lee-chay]
thumbtack una puntina [poon-*tee*-nah]
thunder *(noun)* il tuono [tw*o*h-noh]
  thunderstorm il temporale [−r*ah*-lay]
Thursday giovedì [jo-vay-d*ee*]
ticket il biglietto [beel-*yet*-toh]
  ticket office l'ufficio prenotazioni [oof-*fee*-choh
  pray-no-ta-tzee-*oh*-nee]
  (cloakroom) lo scontrino [skon-*tree*-noh]
» *TRAVEL TIP: see* **bus**
tie *(necktie)* la cravatta
tight *(clothes)* stretto
  they're too tight sono troppo stretti
time il tempo
  what time is it? che ore sono? [kay *oh*-ray . . .]
  I haven't got time non ho tempo [. . . o . . .]
  for the time being per ora
  this time/last time/next time questa volta/la
  volta scorsa/la prossima [pros-see-mah] volta
  3 times tre volte [tray-*vol*-tay]
  have a good time! si diverta! [see dee-v*e*r-tah]
  timetable l'orario [o-r*ah*-ree-oh]
» *TRAVEL TIP: how to tell the time*
  it's one o'clock è l'una [eh l*oo*-nah]
  it's two/three/four o'clock sono le
  due/tre/quattro [lay d*oo*-ay/tray . . .]
  it's 5/10/20/25 past seven sono le sette e
  cinque/dieci/venti/venticinque [s*et*-tay ay ch*ee*n-
  kway/dee-*eh*-chee/v*ay*n-tee/vayn-tee-ch*ee*n-kway]
  it's quarter past eight/eight fifteen sono le
  otto e un quarto/le otto e quindici
  [. . . kw*ee*n-dee-chee]
  it's half past nine/nine thirty sono le nove e
  mezza/le nove e trenta [. . . n*o*-vay ay
  m*et*-tzah . . .]
  it's 25/20/10/5 to ten sono le dieci meno
  venticinque/venti/dieci/cinque [. . . m*ay*-noh . . .]
  it's quarter to eleven/10:45 sono le undici
  meno un quarto/le dieci e quarantacinque
  [*oo*n-dee-chee . . .]

it's twelve o'clock (a.m./p.m.) sono le dodici
(di mattina/di notte) [. . . d*oh*-dee-chee . . . −tay]
at one o'clock all'una
at three thirty alle tre e trenta
tip *(noun)* la mancia [m*an*-chah]
  is the tip included? è compresa la mancia?
  [eh . . .]
» *TRAVEL TIP: same people as in US*
tirare pull
tire la gomma
  I need a new tire ho bisogno di una nuova
  gomma [o bee-s*onn*-yoh dee *oo*-nah
  nw*o*-vah . . .]
» *TRAVEL TIP: tire pressures*

lb/sq in	18	20	22	24	26	28	30
kg/sq cm	1.3	1.4	1.5	1.7	1.8	2	2.1

tired stanco
  I'm tired sono stanco
tissues i fazzolettini di carta
  [ee fat-tzoh-let-*tee*-nee dee . . .]
to: to Rome/England a Roma/in Inghilterra
  [. . . een-gheel-*ter*-rah]
toast il pane tostato [p*ah*-nay tos-t*ah*-toh]
  (drinking) un brindisi [br*een*-dee-see]
» *TRAVEL TIP: "toast" or "tosti" in Italy are*
  toasted sandwiches available as a snack in
  most bars
tobacco il tabacco
tobacco shop il tabaccaio [ta-bak-*kah*-yoh]
» *TRAVEL TIP: stamps can be bought here*
today oggi [*o*-jee]
toe il dito del piede [d*ee*-toh del pee-*eh*-day]
together insieme [een-see-*ay*-may]
  we're together siamo insieme
  [see-*ah*-moh . . .]
  can we pay all together? possiamo pagare
  tutti insieme? [. . . pa-g*ah*-ray . . .]
toilet la toilette [twa-let]
  where are the toilets? dove sono le toilette
  [d*oh*-vay s*oh*-noh lay twa-let]

....

I have to go to the toilet devo andare al gabinetto [d*a*y-voh an-d*a*h-ray . . .]

there's no toilet paper non c'è carta igienica [non cheh k*a*r-tah ee-j*a*y-nee-kah]

men's room uomini

ladies' room donne

» *TRAVEL TIP: only written: ask for* la toilette [twa-let]

public restroom la toilette [twa-let]

» *TRAVEL TIP: most bars have a toilet that can be used free of charge*

tomato un pomodoro

tomato juice il succo di pomodoro [s*oo*k-koh dee . . .]

tomorrow domani [dom-mah-nee]

tomorrow morning/tomorrow afternoon/tomorrow evening domattina/domani pomeriggio [. . . po-may-r*ee*-joh]/domani sera

the day after tomorrow dopodomani

see you tomorrow a domani

ton una tonnellata

» *TRAVEL TIP: 1 ton = 1,016 kilos*

tongue la lingua [l*ee*n-gwah]

tonic (water) l'acqua brillante [. . . breel-l*a*n-tay]

tonight stasera [stah-s*a*y-rah]

tonsillitis la tonsillite [−l*ee*-tay]

tonsils le tonsille [ton-s*ee*l-lay]

too troppo

(also) anche [*a*n-kay]

that's too much questo è troppo [. . . eh . . .]

tool un attrezzo [at-tr*e*t-tzoh]

tooth un dente [d*e*n-tay]

I've got a toothache ho mal di denti [o . . . dee d*e*n-tee]

toothbrush lo spazzolino da denti [spat-tzo-l*ee*-noh . . .]

toothpaste il dentifricio [den-tee-fr*ee*-choh]

top: on top of sopra

on the top floor all'ultimo piano [al-l*oo*l-tee-moh pee-*a*h-noh]

at the top in cima [een chee-mah]

total (noun) il totale [toh-tah-lay]

tough (meat) duro [doo-roh]

tour (noun) un viaggio [vee-ah-joh]
    we'd like to go on a tour of... vorremmo
    visitare... [... vee-see-tah-ray]
    package tour il viaggio organizzato
    [vee-ah-joh or-ga-neet-tzah-toh]

tourist un turista
    I'm a tourist sono un turista
    tourist office l'ufficio turistico [off-fee-choh
    too-rees-tee-koh]

tow (verb) rimorchiare [ree-mor-kee-ah-ray]
    can you give me a tow? mi può rimorchiare?
    [mee pwoh...]
    towrope un cavo da rimorchio [kah-voh dah
    ree-mor-kee-oh]

towards verso
    he was coming straight towards me veniva
    diritto verso di me [vay-nee-vah dee-reet-toh
    ver-soh dee may]

towel un asciugamano [a-shoo-ya-mah-noh]

town la città [cheet-tah]
    in town in città
    would you take me into the town? mi porta
    in città? [mee...]

traditional tradizionale [tra-dee-tzee-o-nah-lay]
    a traditional Italian meal un pasto
    all'italiana

traffic il traffico [traf-fee-koh]
    traffic lights il semaforo [say-mah-fo-roh]
  » TRAVEL TIP: traffic lights are often suspended
    over junctions, so watch out for this
    traffic policeman il vigile [vee-jee-lay]

trailer la roulotte [−lot]

train il treno
    by train col treno
  » TRAVEL TIP: best to reserve in advance as trains
    are crowded; "rapido" is fast intercity, often
    first-class only, surcharge payable

tranquilizers i tranquillanti [−tee]

translate tradurre [tra-door-ray]
   would you translate that for me? me lo può
   trandurre? [may lo pwoh . . .]
transmission *(of car)* la trasmissione
   [tras-mees-*yoh*-nay]
travel: we're traveling around facciamo il giro
   del paese [fa-ch*ah*-moh eel *jee*-roh del
   pah-*ay*-say]
travel agency l'agenzia di viaggi [a-jen-tz*ee*-ah
   dee vee-*ah*-jee]
traveler's check il traveller's cheque
tree l'albero [*al*-bay-roh]
tremendous formidabile [−d*ah*-bee-lay]
trim: just a trim, please solo una spuntatina,
   per favore [. . . spoon-ta-t*ee*-nah . . .]
trip *(noun)* un viaggio [vee-*ah*-joh]
   we want to go on a trip to . . . vorremmo
   fare una gita a . . . [. . . f*ah*-ray *oo*-nah *jee*-tah
   ah]
   have a good trip! buon viaggio! [bwon . . .]
trouble *(noun)* undisturbo [dees-t*oor*-boh]
   **I'm having trouble with the steering/my
   back** ho delle noie allo sterzo/dei disturbi alla
   schiena [o del-lay no-yay *al*-loh st*ay*r-tzoh/day
   dees-t*oor*-bee *al*-lah skee-*ay*-nah]
trousers i pantaloni
truck l'autocarro [ow-toh-k*ar*-roh]
   truck driver il camionista
true vero [v*ay*-ro]
   it's not true non è vero [. . . eh . . .]
trunk *(car)* il portabagagli [por-ta-ba-g*al*-yee]
trunks *(swimming)* il costume [kos-too-may]
trust: I trust you ho fiducia in lei
   [o fee-*doo*-chah een lay]
try *(verb)* provare [pro-v*ah*-ray]
   can I try? posso provare? [. . . pro-v*ah*-ray]
   please try provi per favore [pro-vee payr
   fa-v*oh*-ray]
   can I try it on? posso provarlo?
T-shirt una maglietta [mal-y*ay*t-tah]
Tuesday martedì [mar-tay-d*ee*]

turn: where do we turn off? dove voltiamo?
  [do*h*-vay vol-tee-*ah*-moh]
  he turned without indicating ha voltato
  senza indicare [ah . . . sen-tzah een-dee-k*ah*-ray]
twice due volte [d*oo*-ay vol-tay]
  twice as much il doppio [dop-pee-oh]
twin beds due letti [d*oo*-ay l*e*t-tee]
two due [d*oo*-ay]
typewriter la macchina da scrivere
  [m*a*k-kee-nah dah skr*ee*-vay-ray]
typical tipico [t*ee*-pee-koh]
ugly brutto [br*oo*t-toh]
ulcer l'ulcera [ool-ch*a*y-rah]
umbrella l'ombrello
uncle lo zio [tz*ee*-oh]
uncomfortable scomodo [sko-mo-doh]
unconscious inconscio [een-k*o*n-shoh]
under sotto
underdone poco cotto
underground *(rail)* la metropolitana
understand: I understand capisco [ka-pee-skoh]
  I don't understand non capisco
  do you understand? capisce? [ka-p*ee*-shay]
underwear *(shorts)* le mutande
  [moo-tan-d*ee*-nay]
undo disfare [dees-f*ah*-ray]
unfriendly scontroso
unhappy infelice [een-fay-l*ee*-chay]
United States gli Stati Uniti [lee st*ah*-tee
  oo-n*ee*-tee]
unleaded senza piombo [s*e*n-tzah pee-ombo]
unlock aprire [a-pr*ee*-ray]
until fino a [f*ee*-noh ah]
  not until non prima di [. . . dee]
unusual insolito [een-s*o*-lee-toh]
uomini gentlemen
up su [soo]
  he's not up yet non si è ancora alzato [non
  see eh an-k*o*h-rah al-tz*ah*-toh]
  what's up? cosa succede? [. . . soo-ch*a*y-day]
upside down alla rovescia [. . . ro-v*eh*-shah]

....

upstairs di sopra [dee . . .]
urgent urgente [oor-jen-tay]
us: it's not for us non è per noi [. . . eh payr no-ee]; **can you help us?** può aiutarci? [pwoh ah-yoo-tar-chee]
uscita exit
use: can I use . . . ? posso adoperare . . . ? [rah-ray]
useful utile [oo-tee-lay]
usual solito [so-lee-toh]
  as usual come al solito [koh-may . . .]
usually di solito [dee . . .]
U-turn un'inversione [een-vers-yoh-nay]
vacancy: do you have any vacanies? avete una camera libera? [a-vay-tay oo-nah kah-may-rah lee-bay-rah]
vacate *(room)* lasciare vacante [la-shah-ray va-kan-tay]
vacation una vacanza [va-kan-tzah]
  I'm on vacation sono in vacanza
vaccination la vaccinazione [va-chee-na-tzee-oh-nay]
valanghe avalanches
valid valido [vah-lee-doh]
  how long is it valid for? fino a quando è valido? [fee-noh ah . . .]
valuable di valore [dee va-loh-ray]
  my valuables i miei oggetti di valore [ee mee-eh-ee o-jet-tee . . .]
value *(noun)* valore [va-loh-ray]
valve la valvola [val-vo-lah]
vanilla la vaniglia [va-neel-yah]
varicose veins le vene varicose [vay-nay va-ree-koh-say]
veal il vitello [vee-tel-loh]
vegetables le verdure [vayr-doo-ray]
vegetarian *(noun)* un vegetariano [vay-jay-ta-ree-ah-noh]
ventilator il ventilatore [−toh-ray]
vernice fresca wet paint
very molto

very much moltissimo
via via [vee-ah]
vietato fumare *no smoking*
village il villaggio [veel-lah-joh]
vine la vite [vee-tay]
vinegar l'aceto [a-chay-toh]
vineyard la vigna [veen-yah]
vintage l'annata
violent violento [vee-o-len-toh]
visibility la visibilità [−tah]
visit *(verb)* visitare [vee-see-tah-ray]
vodka la vodka
voice la voce [voh-chay]
voltage il voltaggio [vol-tah-joh]
waist la vita [vee-tah]

» *TRAVEL TIP: waist measurements*

US	24	26	28	30	32	34	36	38
Italy	61	66	71	76	80	87	91	97

wait: will we have to wait long? dobbiamo aspettare a lungo? [. . . as-payt-tah-ray ah loon-goh]
   wait for me mi aspetti [mee . . .]
   I'm waiting for a friend/my wife aspetto un amico/mia moglie [. . . oon a-mee-koh/mee-ah-mol-yay]
waiter il cameriere [ka-may-ree-eh-ray]
   waiter! cameriere!
waitress la cameriera [ka-may-ree-eh-rah]
   waitress! cameriera!
wake: will you wake me at 7:30? mi sveglia alle sette e mezza? [mee svel-yah al-lay set-tay ay met-tzah]
Wales il Galles [gal-lays]
walk: can we walk there? possiamo andarci a piedi? [. . . an-dar-chee ah pee-eh-dee]
   are there any good walks around here? ci sono delle belle passeggiate qua? [chee soh-noh del-lay bel-lay pas-say-jah-tay kwa]
   walking shoes le scarpe da passeggio [lay skar-pay dah pas-say-joh]

....

wall il muro [m*oo*-roh]
  (inside) la parete [pa-r*ay*-tay]
wallet il portafoglio [por-ta-fol-yoh]
want: I want a... voglio un [v*ol*-yoh oon]
  I want to talk to... voglio parlare con...
  [...par-l*ah*-ray...]
  what do you/does he want? che cosa vuole?
  [kay-k*o*-sah vw*o*-lay]
  I don't want to non ne ho voglia [non nay o
  v*ol*-yah]
warm caldo
warning l'avviso [av-v*ee*-soh]
was: I was/he was ero/era [*eh*-roh...]
  it was era
wash: can you wash these for me? può
  lavarmi questi? [pwoh...]
  where can I wash? dove mi posso lavare?
  [d*oh*-vay mee...la-v*ah*-ray]
  where can I wash this? dove posso lavare
  questo?
  washing machine la lavatrice
  [la-va-tr*ee*-chay]
washer *(for nut & bolt)* la rondella
wasp la vespa
watch *(wrist-)* l'orologio [o-ro-l*oh*-joh]
  will you watch my bags for me? può
  guardarmi i bagagli? [pwoh gwar-d*ar*-mee ee
  ba-g*al*-yee]
  watch out! attento!
water l'acqua
  can I have some water? posso avere
  dell'acqua? [...a-v*ay*-ray...]
  hot and cold running water acqua corrente
  calde e fredda [...kor-r*en*-tay...]
  waterproof impermeabile
  [eem-per-may-*ah*-bee-lay]
  waterskiing lo sci nautico [shee n*ow*-tee-koh]
**way: we'd like to eat the Italian
  way** vorremmo mangiare all'italiana [...man-
  j*ah*-ray...]
  could you tell me the way to...? mi può

indicare la strada per ...? [mee pwoh
een-dee-k*ah*-ray ...]
see **where** *for answers*

we noi [n*o*-ee]
   we are siamo [see-*ah*-moh]

weak *(person)* debole [d*ay*-bo-lay]

weather il tempo
   what lousy weather! che tempo schifoso! [kay
tem-poh skee-f*oh*-soh]
   what's the weather forecast? quali sono le
previsioni del tempo? [kw*ah*-lee s*oh*-noh lay
pray-vee-see-*oh*-nee ...]
YOU MAY THEN HEAR...
   pioverà [pee-o-vay-r*ah*] *it is going to rain*
   farà bel tempo [fa-r*ah* ...] *it's going to be
fine*

Wednesday mercoledì [mer-ko-lay-d*ee*]

week la settimana
   a week from today oggi a otto [*o*-jee ...]
   at the weekend al weekend

weight il peso

well: I'm not feeling well non mi sento bene
[non mee sen-toh b*ay*-nay]
   he's not well non sta bene
   how are you?–very well, thanks come sta?
–bene, grazie [k*oh*-may stah – b*ay*-nay
gr*ah*-tzee-ay]
   you speak English very well parla un buon
inglese [... bwon een-gl*ay*-say]

Welsh gallese [gal-l*ay*-say]

were: you were era [*eh*-rah]
   (familiar) eri
   (plural) eravate [eh-ra-v*ah*-tay]
   we were eravamo
   they were erano [*eh*-ra-noh]

west ovest [*o*-vest]

West Indies le Indie Occidentali [*een*-dee-ay
o-chee-dayn-t*ah*-lee]

wet bagnato [ban-y*ah*-toh]
   (weather) umido [*oo*-mee-doh]
   wet suit la tuta da sub [*too*-tah dah soob]

....

what cosa
  what is that? cos'è questo? [koh-*seh* . . .]
  what for? perché [payr-k*ay*]
wheel la ruota [rwo-tah]
wheelchair una poltrona da invalido
  [. . . een-v*ah*-lee-doh]
when quando
  when is breakfast? a che ora è la colazione?
  [ah kay *oh*-rah eh lah ko-la-tzee-*oh*-nay]
where dove [d*oh*-vay]
  where is the post office? dov'è l'ufficio
  postale? [doh-v*eh* loof-f*ee*-choh pos-t*ah*-lay]
  YOU MAY THEN HEAR . . .
  diritto *straight ahead*
  a destra *to the right*
  a sinistra *to the left*
  torni in dietro *go back*
which quale [kw*ah*-lay]
  which one? quale
  YOU MAY THEN HEAR . . .
  questo *this one* quello *that one*
whisky il whisky
white bianco
who chi [kee]
wholesale all'ingrosso
whose di chi [dee kee]
  whose is this? di chi è questo?
  YOU MAY THEN HEAR . . .
  è mio *it's mine*
  è suo *it's his/it's hers*
why perché [payr-k*ay*]
  why not? perché no?
wide largo
wife: my wife mia moglie [m*ee*-ah m*o*l-yay]
will: when will it be finished? quando sarà
  pronto?
  will you do it? lo fa lei? [. . . lay]
  I will come back tomorrow torno domani
wind *(noun)* il vento
window la finestra [fee-n*es*-trah]

....

near the window vicino alla finestra
[vee-ch*ee*-noh . . .]

windshield il parabrezza [pa-ra-br*ay*t-tzah]
  windshield wipers i tergicristalli
  [ee tayr-jee-krees-t*a*l-lee]

windy: it is windy today oggi c'è vento [o-jee
cheh ven-toh]

wine il vino [*vee*-noh]
  can I see the wine list? posso avere la lista
  dei vini? [. . . a-v*ay*-ray lah l*ee*s-tah day v*ee*-nee]

» *TRAVEL TIP: best wines show D.O.C.*
  (Demoninazione d'Origine Controllata) and the
  place where bottled (cantine di . . .) on the
  label;

Barolo, Barbera, Barbaresco full bodied reds
  from Piedmont, go well with roasts and
  venison;

Bardolino, Valpolicella light reds, go well with all
  kinds of meat;

Pinot Bianco/Grigio dry whites from Friuli;

Lambrusco sparkling red from Emilia;

Frascati white, dry or sweet, from near Rome;

Chianti red and white, from Tuscany, (the best is
  Chianti Classico);

Verdicchio dry white from Marche, very good
  with fish;

Vernaccia dry white from Sardinia, very strong
  and aromatic

winter l'inverno

wire il filo metallico [f*ee*-loh may-t*a*l-lee-koh]
  (electrical) il filo eletrico

wish: best wishes tanti auguri

with con

without senza [s*en*-tzah]

witness testimone [tes-tee-m*oh*-nay]
  will you be a witness for me? mi può fare
  da testimone? [mee pwoh f*ah*-ray . . .]

woman la donna

women le donne [d*on*-nay]

wonderful meraviglioso [may-ra-veel-y*oh*-soh]

won't: it won't start no parte [−tay]
wood *(trees)* il bosco
   it's made of wood è di legno [eh di l*ay*n-yoh]
wool la lana
word la parola
   I don't know that word non conosco quella
   parola
work *(verb)* lavorare [la-vo-r*ah*-ray]
   it's not working non funziona
   [. . . foon-tzee-*oh*-nah]
   I work in London lavoro a Londra
worry: I'm worried about him sono
   preoccupato per lui [. . . l*oo*-ee]
   don't worry non si preoccupi
worse: it's worse è peggio [eh p*eh*-joh]
   he's getting worse sta peggiorando [stah
   pay-jo-r*a*n-doh]
worst il peggio [p*eh*-joh]
worth: it's not worth that much non vale tanto
   [. . . v*ah*-lay . . .]
   is it worthwhile going to . . . ? vale la pena
   di andare a . . . ? [v*ah*-lay lah p*ay*-nah dee
   an-d*ah*-ray ah]
wrap: could you wrap it up? mi può fare un
   pacchetto? [mee pwoh f*ah*-ray oon-pak-k*ay*t-toh]
wrench *(noun: tool)* la chiave inglese [kee-*ah*-vay
   een-gl*ay*-say]
wrist il polso
write scrivere [skr*ee*-vay-ray]
   could you write it down? può scriverlo?
   [pwoh . . .]
   I'll write to you ti scrivo [tee skr*ee*-voh]
   writing paper la carta da lettere
   [. . . l*et*-tay-ray]
wrong sbagliato [sbal-y*ah*-toh]
   I think the bill's wrong penso che il conto
   sia sbagliato
   there's something wrong with . . . c'è
   qualcosa che non va con . . . [cheh kwal-*ko*-sa
   kay . . .]
   you're wrong lei ha torto [lay ah t*or*-toh]

sorry, wrong number scusi, ho sbagliato numero [skoo-zee, o sbal-yah-toh noo-may-roh]

X-ray una radiografia [ra-dee-o-gra-fee-ah]

yacht lo yacht

yard *(measurement)* una iarda [yar-dah]

» *TRAVEL TIP: 1 yard = 91.44 cm = 0.91 m*

year l'anno

this year/next year quest'anno/l'anno prossimo [. . . pros-see-moh]

yellow giallo [jal-loh]

yes sì [see]

yesterday ieri [yeh-ree]

the day before yesterday l'altroieri [al-tro-yeh-ree]

yesterday morning/afternoon ieri mattina/ieri pomeriggio [. . . po-may-ree-joh]

yet: is it ready yet? è già pronto? [eh djah . . .]

not yet non ancora

yogurt lo yoghurt

you lei [lay]

(familiar) tu [too]

(plural) voi [vo-ee]

I can't hear you non la/ti/vi sento [. . . tee vee . . .]

I'll send it to you glielo spedisco [lee-ay-loh . . .]/te lo spedisco [tay . . .]/ve lo spedisco [vay . . .]

with you con lei/te/voi

is that you? è lei/sei tu/siete voi? [eh lay/say too/see-ay-tay vo-ee]

» *TRAVEL TIP: only use the "tu" form with good friends*

young giovane [joh-va-nay]

your suo [soo-oh]; tuo [too-oh]; vostro

see **you**

is this your camera, is this yours? è questa la sua/tua macchina fotografica, è sua/tua questa? [eh . . . mak-kee-nah photo-grah-fee-kah . . .]

youth hostel l'ostello per la gioventù [. . . jo-ven-too]

Yugoslavia la Jugoslavia [yoo-go...]
Yugoslavian jugoslavo
zero zero [tz*eh*-roh]
   below zero sotto zero
zipper la cerniera [chayr-nee-*eh*-rah]
zona disco parking permit zone

The Italian Alphabet
letters in parentheses don't actually exist in the Italian alphabet but are useful for spelling English names, etc.

a [ah]
b [bee]
c [chee]
d [dee]
e [ay]
f [effay]
g [gee]
h [akka]
i [ee]
(j) [ee lunga]
(k) [kappa]
l [ellay]
m [emmay]
n [ennay]
o [oh]
p [pee]
q [koo]
r [erray]
s [essay]
t [tee]
u [oo]
v [voo]
(w) [voo doppio]
(x) [eeks]
(y) [ee-greka]
z [tzay-tah]

Numbers

0 zero [tzay-roh]

1 uno [*oo*-noh]	6 sei [say]
2 due [*doo*-ay]	7 sette [*set*-tay]
3 tre [tray]	8 otto
4 quattro	9 nove [*no*-vay]
5 cinque [ch*een*-kway]	10 dieci [dee-*eh*-chee]

11 undici [*oon*-dee-chee]
12 dodici [d*oh*-dee-chee]
13 tredici [tr*ay*-dee-chee]
14 quattordici [kwat-tor-dee-chee]
15 quindici [kw*een*-dee-chee]
16 sedici [s*ay*-dee-chee]
17 diciassette [dee-chas-*set*-tay]
18 diciotto [dee-ch*ot*-toh]
19 diciannove [dee-chan-*no*-vay]

20 venti	21 ventuno
22 ventidue	23 ventitré
24 ventiquattro	25 venticinque
26 ventisei	27 ventisette
28 ventotto	29 ventinove

30 trenta	31 trentuno
40 quaranta	50 cinquanta
60 sessanta	70 settanta
80 ottanta	90 novanta

100 cento [ch*en*-toh]
101 centouno [ch*en*-toh-*oo*-noh]
165 centosessantacinque
200 duecento
1000 mille [m*ee*l-lay]
2000 duemila [doo-ay-m*ee*-lah]